SOUTHERN AFRICA
WHAT KIND OF CHANGE?

PETER HANNON

SOUTHERN AFRICA
WHAT KIND OF CHANGE?

GROSVENOR BOOKS

P.O. BOX 10144 JOHANNESBURG 2000

Further copies available from:

Grosvenor Books, P.O. Box 10144, Johannesburg 2000

Telephone: Johannesburg 23-1697

1st Edition February 1977
2nd Edition April 1977

Printed by Citadel Press, Lansdowne, Cape

CONTENTS

1. WHAT KIND OF CHANGE?

I love South Africa. Some hate it. Most who live there and most who look at it as outsiders would agree that change is needed and is bound to come. The same is true for Rhodesia where my wife was born. The unanswered question is: what kind of change will it be? On that depends the freedom and security of millions.

To take sides, for or against this group or that group, is facile. I come from Northern Ireland, so I have no basis for self-righteous judgement of any other country, whatever the rights or wrongs. In our city streets and country lanes, bullets and bombs, killings and maimings are the price we pay for unanswered prejudices and hates.

It is the very need of countries like my own which makes me want to write about Southern Africa. For I believe it is possible that from the tip of this vast continent there could be mined, not just gold or uranium, but something of even greater value – the cure to that which divides man from man.

That is a bold thing to say. There are few places where one meets such division. As I write these words a pall of smoke hangs over Soweto, and in Cape Town, where I am living, killings are becoming chillingly commonplace when rioters roam the streets.

There are no neutrals in Southern Africa for everyone has within them the instinctive reactions which are the stuff of conflict. Passionate points of view prevail, from the black man who is convinced that time is on his side, to the white man who fears the future and is sure that he is damned if he loses control.

Southern Africa, too, is a focus of international issues and interests. Because of its institutionalised division it is used to highlight the clash between white and non-white, between 'have' and 'have not', between imperialist and colonised, between the industrialised and the 'third' worlds everywhere.

The natural self-interest of the great powers adds to this. Envious eyes are cast on the area's mineral resources and on the strategic importance of the Cape sea route which links Europe to its oil supplies.

In the space of twenty four hours recently I met two men who summed up opposite sides within South Africa. The first was a militantly bitter brown leader who laid the death of his father at the white man's door. "The Government's so-called new policy means absolutely nothing," he said. "Only bloody revolution will break the structure of exploitation." You may agree or disagree with him. That is not the point. The point is that he is an inescapable factor in the equation.

The second was a white businessman who said, "When the chips are down it is only power that counts. We must be sure that we build up and keep the decisive power in our hands. That is our only hope."

These men are, in fact, the reverse sides of the same coin. Each implies that people's motives can never change fundamentally enough. The selfish will always hold what they have or grab what they haven't. It is the law of the jungle. Each, however, leaves several questions unanswered.

One is: How can we be sure that the oppressed, when he comes to power, does not in turn become the oppressor, thereby perpetuating the exploitation of man by man?

Another is: How can the white man, a tiny minority in a

black continent, move beyond resisting for as long as possible the inevitable pressure of a vast black majority? He may do it for a generation. But, on that basis, what future can he offer his children and grandchildren?

White and black face two further questions. Is the black man, in his determination to see change, going to become the victim of exploitation by those who will use him for their own, quite different ends? One hears voices which say, "Our aim is to create a Marxist state!" 'One man, one vote', or the wishes of the majority of their own people seem to take second place in such people's calculations. Their interest is power. Where, one might ask, does that differ in motive from their picture of those they want to overthrow?

I write this in November, 1976. President Nyerere of Tanzania is reported as saying that it is preferable for anyone to live in a country ill-run by his own people than well-run by someone else. One understands his point, but it would be sad if that became the only alternative.

For the white man there is another dilemma. He sees Communism's bid for his country and rejects it. But mere anti-Communism serves the Communist purpose. Any trained ideologist in Moscow or Peking must rub his hands in delight at anti-Communist pronouncements from white Southern Africa because it pushes the disaffected non-whites everywhere into his camp.

During the Angolan war opinion polls testified that the sympathy of most South African blacks lay with the MPLA. This did not mean that they were pro-Communist. Their instinctive support, however, went to those who "were teaching the white man a lesson".

So how does the white man find a role which does not disarm him, but which will enable him to take an ideological initiative, rather than always be its victim?

Forces of extreme right and left constantly emphasise the wrong dividing lines and exploit them powerfully. They keep reiterating that it is race, colour or class which should and must divide.

What is the right dividing line? Should it not be between those who truly want to build a just society for the benefit of *all* and the exploitation of *none* and those who exploit division for their vested interest of profit or power?

The very depth of feelings in Southern Africa, and the conviction of many that it is an insoluble situation, ensure that if answers can be found to work here, they will be of intense interest elsewhere.

I do not now just speak of political choices, vital though these are. I think, rather, of how people react in a pressure situation, their motives, their compulsions, their aims. These will decide what system evolves. These have universal relevance because they are reproduced in differing circumstances the world over.

You have only to shut your eyes as you hear men and women of Southern Africa express their honest feelings and you can picture yourself listening to Protestant and Catholic in Ireland, Black and White in the United States, French- and English-speaking in Canada, Australian and Aboriginal and so on. The list is endless. I write only of those whom I have met and heard myself.

So we face a universal need. Mankind's capacity to destroy itself has become a commonplace. In the next years it is possible that some dedicated or unbalanced guerilla group will get its hands on nuclear weapons and use them regardless of consequences. Continental famines are imminent. Experts predict ecological disaster. Growing divisions point to failures in capitalism. Productive inefficiency and the merciless persecution of dissidents point to failures in communism.

We face, in fact, the failure of mankind. A new maturity and a new realism must be found or the future for all is bleak.

Is it possible for new motives to emerge which can lead to new ways of living together? Or is it inevitable that man's animal instincts will prevail? This is the supreme issue in Southern Africa. We may dress it up in various phrases – the survival of the fittest; enlightened self-interest; the territorial imperative and so on. They all amount to the same thing – however brilliant we are, however scientifically advanced, intellectually reasonable, or politically educated, we will react like cavemen when basic instincts are aroused and so, without meaning to do so, make destruction inevitable.

A man called Paul, two thousand years ago, put it as clearly as anyone. "My own behaviour baffles me," he wrote. "I often find I have the will to do good, but not the power. That is, I don't accomplish the good that I set out to do, and the evil that I don't really want to do I find I am always doing . . . it is an agonising situation. I thank God there is a way out."

This book is not a political treatise. It is written to tell the true stories of certain men and women of Southern Africa whose experience may point to "the way out". They do not pretend to have ready-made solutions. They do not claim to be unique. There must be many others in these lands with similar rich experience. I write of them because they are people whom I know.

Their significance is not so much their impact on events thus far. Rather, they are prototypes in a laboratory situation, pro-

11

totypes which must be multiplied if realistic solutions are to be found.

The historian, Arnold Toynbee, articulated the concept of "an inspired minority" as the instigators of human progress. This implies that the door to the future can hinge not on the majority, but on the few men and women who, free from the dictatorship of prevailing ways of doing things, go all out to seize the initiative for a new way.

Are these men and women, whose stories follow, initiators of the needed new way? This question is the link between them.

2. WHICH WAY AFRICA?

Why do I say that South Africa could help a country like mine?
Let me give one instance.

July, 1971, was the height of our riot season in Northern
Ireland. Many Irish were asking, "What can we do?". Some
of us in Belfast heard that an unusual group of South Africans
were visiting Europe. They included white farmers, ministers
of the Dutch Reformed Church and black headmasters. Dr.
William Nkomo, who had been one of the founders and became
the first President of the militant African National Congress
Youth League, was one of their main spokesmen.

This group seemed to indicate that it was possible for divided
people to find a uniting purpose. We thought that if the Irish
were no longer prepared to listen to each other, perhaps they
would listen to South Africans. We invited them to Belfast.

Every door was open to them. They were received by our
Government; they had long talks with the Protestant Arch-
bishop and the Catholic Cardinal; they met radical leaders
and grassroots workers.

The South Africans did not say that they had all the answers.
There was no suggestion that all was well in their own country.
They were very open about the need for change. They were,
however, also convinced that change was possible and that the
deepest prejudices, hates and fears could be cured because it
was happening to them individually.

The visitors did not speak about Ireland, but we Irish could
not fail to get the point. The cost of our own pettiness was
vividly brought home by these men from another continent.
We were fascinated.

Dr. Nkomo made a particular impact. One had only to look at his face to know that he spoke from dearly-bought experience. He knew hurt and humiliation. We discovered, for instance, that earlier in the year he had been driving in his home city of Pretoria. Not realising that some roads had been rerouted for a civic occasion, he drove the wrong way up a one-way street. A white policeman, quite rightly, stopped him, but then began abusing him and finally hit him in the face, seriously injuring the sight of an eye. Nkomo took him to court. Just before he was due to leave South Africa for Europe the case came up for trial. The policeman was found guilty but discharged.

Bitterness welled up in Nkomo. It filled his horizon. He said to himself, "We have taken too much to God. This we must take to blood".

For twenty four hours he wrestled with himself. He wanted nothing to do with any white man. Then he decided he was not going to let any other individual's wrongdoing deflect him from what he felt was right. So he came to Belfast.

He was ill, with a weak heart and almost blind. That did not hold him back. He spoke with force to everyone he met. His theme was how to have the needed change go deep enough. It had to deal with prime motives and reactions, otherwise it would be transient and no permanent cure to the exploitation of man by man.

From his early days Nkomo had been in the struggle for the rights of his people. The African newspaper *The World* called him "one of the foremost, outspoken, black leaders". He told us how, in 1953, he had gone to a conference for all races of Southern Africa in Lusaka, Zambia, and how this had been a decisive point for him. He said, "There I saw white men change, I saw black men change, and I myself decided to change." What particularly shook him was the transformation which he saw in what he graphically described as "rabid Afrikaner nationalists."

What did this "change" mean? Nkomo realised that bitterness had made him a prisoner, limiting his vision and distorting his fight. His determination to put right what was wrong now deepened and also broadened to include not just what was needed for his own people but for all races.

At first some of his black friends did not understand and he faced persecution from that side as well as from some whites who did not welcome his outspoken fearlessness. Increasingly, however, people turned to him for leadership. He became the first black President of the Institute of Race Relations. One paper described his indictment of wrong as "a hurricane of fire which shocked people into a new search for freedom". When he died, the year after his visit to Northern Ireland, 10 000 people came to his funeral. An article in the *Rand Daily Mail* was headed "the father of all blacks".

Nkomo had travelled widely. He knew many of the leaders of the new Africa, and elsewhere. On every occasion he spoke for the continent he wanted to see.

"Many people ask, 'Which way will Africa go?' " he said. "At the moment I believe Africa is confused. There is a crisis in character. Men who were united when they fought for the freedom of their continent and countries have now allowed self-interest to take precedence in their lives. Unless we can get an incorruptible type of leader who will not be bought with money, with position, with success and with the promise of other things then Africa will be doomed. Other ideologies are dividing us. We need the ideology that begins when a man listens to God and begins to live by absolute moral standards. Then he need no longer have a blueprint because he needs to know nothing more except to be sure that he lives at the Cross and moves as God guides".

In Ireland we saw how he pursued his aim. He spent much time talking personally with his companions about how to become free from the dishonesties and temptations that can tie a man down and weaken his leadership. His African friends felt his firmness, as did his white colleagues.

There was a young Afrikaans engineering student in the party. Because of Nkomo's bad health and poor eyesight he offered to look after him. He thought that this would mean carrying meals to his room, but soon also found himself polishing his shoes, making his bed, packing his suitcases and even sweeping the floor.

"I hadn't bargained with this", he says now. He began to get worried as to what his family and friends would think if it leaked out that he was doing this for a black man. He was scared of being called a "kaffirboetie". After a few days he said to himself, "Well, I don't have to do this, but I won't chicken out now. I will act nicely here. And when I get home things will return to normal."

It was not long before he saw his hypocrisy, so he told Dr. Nkomo what churned around inside him. He says, "We started talking – or at least I did – about South Africa and I told him what I thought of the political situation there and what ought to be done about the Africans and how their affairs should be run. During this time he was quiet and listened. When I eventually finished he said, "Why do you think you know better than us what's best for me and my people?"

"That made me think, and I realised for the first time that that was the way I treated other people and especially Africans. I had to re-think my whole way of living."

The next day Nkomo asked the young Afrikaner to read for him a chapter from Galatians in the New Testament. He, himself, could not read because of his damaged eyes. Part of it said, "There is no such thing as Jew or Gentile, slave and freeman, male and female; for you are all one person in Christ Jesus". The Afrikaner says, "I don't know whether he did it on purpose or not, but I got the point!"

"Since that time," he goes on, "I have begun to get a new sense of destiny for my own people. Deep down we are aware of spiritual things. So is the African. Why are we here together in Africa? We Afrikaners may need to learn that it takes more grace to receive than to give. We need to learn from other people. If we do this, then we can be used to build bridges between people who are divided. Our part as white people cannot be isolated from the rest of the continent. Many of us are afraid and feel at the mercy of events. But we can choose to be part of a new role for the continent".

As they cared for a country like mine the South Africans realised increasingly what an unrivalled asset their own varied background was. It was a fresh concept. Where many regard South Africa's diversity as an insuperable obstacle, here it was being put humbly yet effectively at the service of other nations.

One of the most senior Churchmen in Ireland said to Nkomo, "Would it help if I came out publicly condemning what I cannot agree with in South Africa?"

Nkomo was silent for a moment and then said, "Your Eminence, we have not come here to tell anyone what to do or not to do. You must do what you feel is right. May I tell you what we have found most helpful? Some people came to South Africa from Europe. They won our trust, both black and white. They helped us face the things that were wrong in our lives; they helped us put these things right; they helped us hand over control of our lives to God and to listen to Him. That is why we can be here today united as white and black South Africans.

"Your Eminence, could you help some Catholics and Protestants in Ireland find that same unity and then encourage them to come and help us?"

Day after day Nkomo encouraged the South Africans to use all they were learning in their own lives to get through to the hearts – and to the entrenched viewpoints and prejudices – of the Irish whom they were meeting. It was a crash course in that neglected art of statesmanship – how to turn an enemy into a friend.

3. THE RHODESIAN AND THE ZIMBABWEAN

At two hours' notice five hundred students of the coloured University of the Western Cape jammed into their biggest lecture hall, at the expense of their lunch. The attraction? A simple notice saying that Rev. Arthur Kanodereka, Treasurer General of the African National Council (Muzorewa wing) and Alec Smith, son of the Rhodesian Prime Minister would speak.

The mood was tense. Many in the audience were men of passion. Some had been imprisoned for the strength of their opposition to the South African system. Official student policy was one of no contact with the whites.

All wanted to know what this unusual combination would have to say. What on earth could bring the son of the white Prime Minister and the representative of the black nationalist movement to speak on the same platform? What was the catch? Who was selling out?

Alec Smith spoke first. Still in his twenties like many in the audience, he went straight on to the offensive. He was not there to defend or justify Rhodesia. He was there to challenge the students to join him in building a just society.

"I grew up taking privileges for granted," he said. "I took for granted that black men would serve me, that I would go to university as a right and that I would get a top job."

His listeners sat up at such frankness from one of the white establishment.

"This arrogance and my self-centred indifference to others has been changed," Smith continued. "Now, cost what it may, I am determined to work for a society where men are free of everything which keeps them less than they are meant to be."

He then spelt out what this could mean in personal and national terms. He did not know what the future held. There might be a white government; there might be a black government; or a mixture. That was not the final issue. The question was, what *quality* of government, what *quality* of society would it be? He was determined to work for incorruptible government of whatever colour. This was six months before his father's famous meeting with Dr. Kissinger and Mr. Vorster and the launching of new settlement proposals. As I write no one knows what the outcome will be.

Smith emphasised that he was not interested in propping up the status quo. Of course he wanted peace. In the previous month he had lost three friends, one just a fortnight before. "I know that we cannot go on as we are," he said. "Change has got to come. I have decided to apply first in my own life any change I want to see in another man."

Provocatively he said that political solutions could never be enough. They were necessary. But, to be fruitful, they had to be built on a change in peoples' outlook and attitude. Otherwise one unjust society replaces another.

That got through to his audience which has a lively political awareness. The previous week a cast of coloured students had produced Shakespeare's "Macbeth" transposed to modern Africa. The programme notes asked bluntly, "Is there an analogy between Idi Amin and Macbeth?" These students think in terms of the reality of power. In Alec Smith they sensed some new element. They were not sure that they grasped it all, but they gave him a warm round of applause which in itself was unusual.

As he had spoken one little incident showed just how full the hall was. The pressure of those trying to get in began to move the turntable podium on which Smith stood, and he looked like disappearing in one direction while the students pushed in the other. Loud protests from the packed benches out front saved the day.

Then Rev. Arthur Kanodereka was introduced. He is a senior man, middle-aged, with the grey hairs of experience.

"I know what violence is," he said. "I have lived up on the North East border of my country and have supported the guerillas there. I have seen white men killed and black men killed, and looked at their bodies. I know what oppression is and what it is to suffer. I have been arrested three times by the security forces. But I have come to see that my bitterness was also imprisoning me. That bitterness has now gone. With it has gone any spirit of submission or inferiority. I am now a free man."

Like Smith, he told his audience facts of change in hardcore whites and blacks. He said that it was a totally new factor in his country and that it strengthened the black man in his fight. He himself could now meet anyone without fear.

"We must build a new Zimbabwe," he went on. "It is not just a matter of getting rid of the white man. We, ourselves, must have honesty and unselfishness, not every man climbing over the next to get to the top. It is going to ask a lot from people like you and me. I never thought I could stand here beside the Prime Minister's son. But he has changed. And I have changed. Together we are out to build a new Africa and to care for a world that needs our care."

There was another round of applause. Then the questions began. "It sounds nice, but isn't it just talk?" "Can any system change without violence?" "What do your colleagues think?"

"God is a myth and aren't you just being used to prop up a wrong system?"

It quickly became clear that a dozen men were dominating the questions, often vying with each other to make their points. When time ran out there were boos because no one wanted to stop. Many would have continued till midnight. All the way to the car the visitors were surrounded with more questions. In the following days the discussion went on.

The audience in that lecture hall represented the division among the students themselves. On one hand the militant minority, fired by bitterness and seizing the initiative; men convinced that violence alone could do it. On the other hand the Christian element, in the majority, hoping that change might come without violence but silent and unconvincing when it came to articulating how it could happen. Into this dilemma came Kanodereka and Smith, claiming that neither violence nor the status quo was adequate; that realistic change could be achieved by a third way; and that their experience proved this.

That is quite a proposition. If true, its significance is obvious. So I asked Alec Smith what lay behind what he said.

He had been born and brought up on a farm in Rhodesia, he began. As a child many of his natural playmates were black. Colour was no issue. Then he went to school. One day one of the black children from the farm passed as he was with his schoolfriends. Smith greeted him. Afterwards his friends asked, "Why do you want anything to do with someone like that?" He began to think of black and white as different.

His father was a Member of Parliament, so from an early age he was exposed to politics. Sometimes his friends would suddenly stop seeing him because their parents had sided with

22

different parties. This hurt him and made him wonder how deep these friendships really were.

Then, while he was still at school, his father became Prime Minister. This did not affect him at first. But, before long, he began to notice a change in some of those he met. Some seemed to want his friendship for their own gain. Others automatically hated him because they did not agree with his father. "I became very careful about whom I would call a friend," he said. But what went deepest with him was that, more often than not, when he met people, he would be introduced just as Ian Smith's son, without his own name even being mentioned.

"It made me above all want to be myself," he said. So, at college, he went wild and enjoyed himself with a small group of trusted friends. People began to notice him as a person which was what he wanted.

"I went to university in South Africa to study law, but spent most of my time breaking it," he said. He drank a great deal and took drugs. He got involved in political demonstrations and was warned by the police.

"My philosophy all this time was that everything was all right as long as it did not hurt anyone else. In fact I ended up hurting all those I came in contact with. I was often in the newspapers and I embarrassed my parents a great deal, but I enjoyed this because it made me someone in my own right. People would notice me and recognise me even if they did not like me or my way of life."

His career at university ended in disaster. He turned up for an exam dead drunk and wrote a letter to the professor telling him what a stupid paper it was. He was advised that he would not be allowed back into the law faculty.

Back in Rhodesia he was called up to do his national service in the army. He hated every bit of that year and it did not cure him. He was discharged, filled with hate for the whole system. He felt his life was destroyed and lost hope and ambition, drifting into heavy drug-taking and fantasy. His only reality became the next "trip".

Then Smith was arrested for trying to smuggle drugs into the country. This shook him. He was brought to court, sentenced and given a large fine. He had to find the money or go to gaol so he managed to get a job as a photographer. He enjoyed this work and for the first time felt happy with what he was doing. But it did not solve his personal problems. "It was about this time that I began to search into the concept of God and His existence," he said.

Smith thought for a moment. "It was strange. I picked up a New Testament and began to dip into it. It caught my interest. I began to get a sense of God's guiding hand in my life. I can't explain it. I bumped into a man who invited me to his church. I went. There I was faced with the challenge of Christ on the Cross. I knew I had to do something about it, but could not take the final step. For two weeks I wrestled with my fears of the unknown. Finally I gave my life to God and for the first time felt really free."

He had many things to sort out but his new freedom bubbled over. He felt like stopping people in the street to tell them what he had found. Some must have thought he was a bit crazy.

One immediate result was that he was reconciled with his parents. "They were very happy about the change in me," he said, "but of course I was not always very wise in my enthusiasm. My father once asked me, 'Don't you ever do anything in moderation?'"

Meanwhile events, nationally, were moving fast. On Rhodesia's border Angola and Mozambique were gaining independence. The whole face of Southern Africa was shifting. I asked Smith if there was any relationship in his mind between these events and his very personal experience.

"One important thing happened immediately," he said. "It was as if the scales fell from my eyes. For the first time I began to see the reality of my country and its problems. I wanted to do something about it but did not know how."

It was at this point that he ran into some people who showed him a film about the life of Dr. William Nkomo. What struck him was how Nkomo had set out to cure hatred, prejudice and racial division in his land.

Smith glimpsed a possible link between his new-found faith and the needs of Rhodesia and decided to get involved. "I discovered there was a difference between giving my life to God so that He could sort me out and giving my life to God to work towards establishing His authority in the power structure of our country," he said. "I had no idea how it would work out."

In December 1974, some black and white South Africans joined a number of Rhodesians in Bulawayo to discuss possibilities. Among the group were Sir Cyril Hatty, a Minister of Finance in a previous government, Dr. Elliott Gabellah, Vice-President of the ANC, and Alec Smith. They talked about the situation and asked God for guidance.

Various results followed. During a time of quiet together Sir Cyril Hatty was obviously profoundly moved. Later he said what had so deeply affected him. He had found himself, quite unexpectedly, thinking about Herbert Chitepo who had been the first Rhodesian African to qualify as an advocate and to set up practice in Salisbury. Chitepo was now in voluntary exile in Zambia, where he had become external head of ZANU in Lusaka. Hatty had never personally clashed with him, but it was borne in on him that he had been in the Cabinet of Southern Rhodesia at the time when Chitepo had decided that there was no place for him in the scheme of things in Rhodesia and had left the country.

Hatty felt that, as a member of the Cabinet, he shared the responsibility for their failure to enlist Chitepo with all his gifts in the building of a united Rhodesia. He also felt impelled to write to Chitepo in Zambia, telling him of his profound sense of failure and to ask for his forgiveness, in the process offering to meet Chitepo in, say, Malawi to deliver his apology in person.

The violent black revolutionary responded wholeheartedly to this humble honesty from a white man in government circles. He wrote Hatty a warm and generous letter which is surely one of the remarkable documents in the history of conflict in Africa.

31 December 1974

Dear Mr. Hatty

It was a great surprise for me to receive your letter; and an even greater one to hear you express apologies for the problems I had to go through during the years when I started and continued to work as an advocate in Salisbury.

While there were many things which hurt me personally, I realised that many were not directed at me as an individual. It was me as a member of the African Community. Those who perpetrated these irksome measures were not acting as individuals either. They acted as part of the White Community.

For these reasons you personally do not owe me an apology, nor do I hold any sense of grievance against you personally.

It was the system, the group attitudes and policies. What drove me out of Rhodesia was not hatred of any particular person or group – racial or religious. I left Rhodesia because I could not live or work within that system. What has inspired me to sacrifice so much of an otherwise promising future, and to live as I do, is not hatred but love – love of a new order of society in Zimbabwe, free from racial oppression or degradation, in which all have an equal voice in deciding the policies, laws and measures under which they are to live.

The best apology, if there was need for any, is the realisation of these goals – the creation of a new society.

Yours sincerely
H.W. Chitepo

In his reply Sir Cyril thanked Chitepo for his letter and went on:

The vision and understanding you have shown is something I, frankly, had not expected and I am most grateful to you for it. Your letter is written from the heart and I shall always treasure it. It gives me great hope for it shows you and I share the same objective – the creation of a new society here, in which all are free.

I believe it was God's guidance that we should communicate; and His guidance that we should seek to work together to bring about the objective.

Men do change when they listen to God, and although there will be many problems and setbacks, I believe this new society will come about if we follow His guidance.

There are many others here who hold this belief and I would like to have your permission to share your letter with a few of my close friends. May I do so?

I pray for you and for the fulfillment of God's plan for us.

Sincerely
Cyril Hatty

Before Chitepo could reply, he was assassinated.

As Hatty, Gabellah, Alec Smith and the others planned together what to do next, the idea came up of holding an international conference in Salisbury the following June as a platform for a new approach to the country's needs.

They were nervous at the size of the job. Many said that major conferences needed at least eighteen months to prepare and that they were crazy to consider it. They estimated they might need $30 000. A financier said, "You won't get $5 000," for sanctions and recession were combining to make money very tight. However Smith and a friend set out to see what they could do. They approached all sorts of people. Their budget finally worked out at $26 000 and when the auditor made up the final accounts he found they had collected $26 000 48 cents!

The opening meeting astonished Smith. A thousand people in Salisbury's biggest hall; the Rhodesian Front officially represented; four of the Cabinet there; Dr. Gabellah of the ANC one of the main speakers, with a number of his Executive in the hall.

"It was the one platform on which these elements agreed," Smith said. In the subsequent week the Rhodesians were able to get perspective from people of twenty six other countries on how change in individuals can be related to national issues.

They also had time to talk over in a fresh atmosphere the feelings which divided them. This honesty was quite a shock to some whites. Many had never heard what the other side really felt. "We had to ask ourselves – what are we living for? What controls us?" Smith said.

I asked him how he assessed the results of the conference. That was difficult to answer. Most valuable, perhaps, were new relationships established privately between men at the centre of decision-making in the country. In such a volatile situation these must be confidential. Men's lives are at risk.

"One thing I can say for sure," remarked Smith, "Arthur Kanodereka and I would never have been working together but for that conference."

Kanodereka had not wanted to go near the conference. "I had heard that Moral Re-Armament was out to soften us nationalists," he said, "Just as later I heard reactionary whites warn that it was Communist. But my wife said, 'Please, darling, go and see what is there.' Maybe she wanted something for me.

Maybe she knew what my bitterness was costing her and her children. So I went."

"My father had been an evangelist. So when I grew up I thought it natural to follow in his footsteps. But his Christ never became my Christ."

Kanodereka had gone to a college which trained only blacks for the ministry, so he saw his ministry as to the blacks alone. He had no contact with whites and wanted none. He felt he was the victim of racial laws.

"I studied history and learnt what the white man had done," he said. "The British may have lifted us up, but then they left us in oppression. I discovered it was a privilege, not a right, for an African even to go to school. I learnt about the division of the land, where a white man got more than the black. I came to think I was licensed to hate. I could read parts of the Bible which I thought justified my anger, and thought it my duty as a minister to take up my people's cause."

He was appointed by the Methodist Church to the North East border area for seven years. When the war broke out there, his sympathies lay with the guerilla fighters. He felt their cause was his cause.

At times he disagreed with them. Once they attacked a village and killed a pregnant woman. This, he was convinced, was wrong. He preached against them. Then he heard they were after him for what he had said. He knew where their camp was, so he went to them and said, "Here I am." They argued it out.

The security forces arrested him three times for his involvement, but that did not change him. He said that it only fed his bitterness. But, sometimes, when he saw the dead bodies of black and white he was compelled to pray and ask himself, "Is this what God wants?"

Kanodereka was transferred back to the African township of Harare in Salisbury and found himself at the conference. He sat at the back, watched and listened. At first he said nothing. "All I can say," he went on, "is that suddenly my father's Christ became my Christ. I picked up a vision of what could happen. I saw Christ, the suffering Christ, not just for blacks or for whites, but for all people. A care for white people, that they should find something new, came into my heart. I felt a new authority from God to give His message to all people."

Colour stopped being a problem. People became people to him. He became free and without fear. Previously he would tell whites what he thought they wanted to hear, but when they were gone he would laugh with his friends and talk quite differently.

His new ideas were quickly put to the test. That very weekend thirteen people in his township of Harare were shot by the police during a riot. "You can think how our people felt," he said. "Yet I invited Alec to come to my church to talk to my congregation. It was a risk for me. By inviting the son of the Prime Minister at that time I seemed to be asking for trouble. There were young men there who thought violence the only thing. I was afraid."

"So was I," interjected Smith. "As I sat down I looked to see how many people were between me and the door in case I had to make a quick getaway!"

"But Alec was bold enough to come," continued Kanodereka. "I introduced him as a friend and as a changed white man. The people cheered when he told them his story. The whole atmosphere became different."

One naturally wondered what Kanodereka's colleagues thought of what he was doing. "At first, when I told them I could not support violence, they answered, 'We must use the Devil to cross the river. We can leave him when we get to the other side.' I said, 'That is no good. We will not be able to leave him then and our people will suffer.' Well, they were not sure. But they have watched me and seen what I believe in and how I go on, and now more of them are with me. And I am now Treasurer General!"

With the help of their own people, Kanodereka and Smith raised money to travel to Europe together. They went to the Moral Re-Armament conference at Caux in Switzerland. They met delegates to the World Council of Churches in Geneva, and talked with groups of exiles in London. In Bern, Kanodereka was asked to meet diplomats interested in Rhodesia. They told him, "Come on your own so that we can speak freely." He said, "I come with Alec Smith or not at all."

In their talks they went beyond political discussion to introduce the idea that no-one seriously concerned for Rhodesia could bypass the need for change in individual people and their aims and attitudes. Some saw the point, some did not. No one, however, could deny that a new factor was coming into the situation.

Kanodereka did not only act on the level of national affairs. Fresh truth grew in other spheres. Much of his forcefulness today springs from what has happened in his family. His hate of the white man had spread into his home and damaged his wife and children. He found that you cannot control hate. He called them together and told them he was sorry. It was a difficult step, but it made his family life quite new. His wife joined him in Switzerland. "We can go together to anyone now because we are solid in our own home," he said.

When Kanodereka returned home he decided that his church

in the heart of that tinder-dry situation of Harare could be the centre of bolder initiative. He invited all who would like to come, from whatever background, to join together each Sunday evening to pray for God's way for their country. When I spoke to him this had been continuing for twelve weeks.

These were no gatherings of the faintly pious. "Some support the fighting in the bush," he said. "Others are in the security forces. Up to seven or eight hundred have come at a time. After three Sundays I had to ask people to give me a mandate to continue. When I put the question, every black and white hand went up together. It moved me very much.

"We are discouraging sermons," he went on with a chuckle. "Sermons can hijack us into quite another spirit. A black clergyman can come and use the chance to air his ideas. A white clergyman can do the same. Before you know it you have more division. No. People need to come to learn to give God the authority in our land."

Three other Executive Members of the ANC have had a part in taking these meetings with Kanodereka.

As one sits in that church just across the road from the massed blocks of hostels for black single workers – often the sparkplug of anti-white or inter-party riots – one is aware of the significance of Kanodereka's leadership week after week. Often young men from one faction come to him, ready to react violently to something done by the other side. Kanodereka says, "I tell them 'Go and talk to the others instead of hitting them. It is more likely to change them.' And they do."

One of the most senior ANC leaders, who meets often with leaders from neighbouring black countries, spoke publicly in Harare alongside Kanodereka. He said that he believed firmly that 'it is God's will that all men can be free.' He forcibly condemned the system running Rhodesia, but said equally forcibly that it will take new men to build a new Zimbabwe, men changed by God from 'crooked ways'.

"Some people talk about government in 'civilised hands', " he said. "Does colour imply civilisation?" (A hearty "No" from his audience). "In London you get as good devils as here. A government remaining in civilised hands which implies white hands is not right. It is a government by the people, perhaps governed by God, that is the government which I would like. It is not white government. It is not black government. We have black governments in Africa and in some countries you cannot say what I am saying here. That is not what we want. 'The truth shall make you free.' "

Such outspokenness from a man at one of the world's pressure points, where assassination is not unknown, takes courage.

As one listens to men like Kanodereka and Smith one thing is clear – they do not see themselves engaged in a peace-keeping operation. They want peace. Any sensible man does. But, more than that they are out to bring a change to the society in which they live. They know that a true peace can only come from wrongs being put right.

Talking to white and black leaders alike Kanodereka says, "We have given our lives to God. We listen to Him. We do what He tells us. So we are not prisoners of the white camp or prisoners of the black camp. We are free men."

Alec Smith asks, "Is our faith relevant to the young men who leave their homes, their studies, their jobs to trek 500 miles across the border to join the guerillas? They do not do it because they are bored on a Saturday afternoon. They do not leave because they are Communists. Once across the border they may be influenced by the Cubans, the Russians, the

Chinese. But they remain Rhodesians. They leave because of the frustrations in *our* society. It is too cheap to blame outsiders for our troubles. It is a civil war we are fighting, Rhodesians against Rhodesians. So any cure must come from within ourselves."

4. THE PROFESSOR'S DINNER PARTIES

A professor at the University of Rhodesia returned to Salisbury just before the conference to which Kanodereka went. He and his wife were in deep gloom over the prospects for their country.

The professor himself tells the story:

"I found myself, rather unwillingly I may say, at some of the final sessions of the conference. It was being held on the university campus and my wife had been interested by some of the earlier meetings.

"I have been to many conferences. They are always difficult to evaluate, but this one clearly had its impact. It seemed to come just at the right moment. Some of its implications are still being felt in our country.

"I had recently had an operation and while recovering, lying on my back, the thought had kept recurring in my mind, 'a still, small voice'. At the conference this came back to me. I began to look around to see how to activate in my own sphere what that voice was telling me. I thought of the sphere of influence closest to me, the university.

"One member of my staff happened to be one of the key figures in the African political movement. Was there a way I could begin to work with this man to effect a meeting on a person to person level between extreme right wing members of the Rhodesian Front and various members of the ANC, I pondered? It seemed to me that these two sides had never had a meaningful dialogue.

"There was just one snag. For a long time I had regarded this man as an academic lightweight. So I had never got to know him at all well. I began to realise that this was entirely my fault. I had superimposed a stereotype on him without allowing him to react to me as a person – somehow a miniature of what we were doing all the time with the other racial group.

"One morning, screwing up my courage, I went into his office and said, 'I want to apologise to you for the way I have treated you all this time. I'm afraid I seriously underestimated your academic potential.'

"He is by nature a reticent and retiring man, but his face lit up in a way I had never seen before. From that moment we never looked back. I spoke to him about my plans for these possible meetings. He said he would gladly arrange for me to invite members of the ANC whom I did not know. It was up to me to meet members of the Government. Here I had no idea what to do. I knew several Cabinet Ministers slightly but I thought I must begin on a level I could manage.

"One Monday afternoon I was in my office, very busy. Somehow I received an implicit directive, that was never in words, to go to town. It was most inconvenient. I had a lecture at 4.00 p.m. There was really no time, but something told me to do it.

"I got on my Velosolex and cycled to town, did some business and started to walk the distance to the government buildings. I could not think whom to see except, perhaps, a certain member of the Prime Minister's staff, a man close to him, whom I did not know but had seen on a platform.

"As I walked, suddenly I got a strong imperative to go back, get the bicycle and ride there with all haste instead of walking. So I did this. As I reached the opening to Parliament this very man walked out of the front door.

"I went up to him, introduced myself and said, 'Would you come to a lunch at my house with some members of the ANC?'

"He looked a bit startled. He said, 'It's strange that you

should have caught me now. For the past week I have been away on business and am just now on my way to a passing out parade and will not be back for another three days. You have found me at the only moment you could have done so for quite a long time.'

"So we had that first lunch. I was nervous. There was no agenda. I just wanted those who came to meet as human beings and not as faceless cyphers over a conference table. Somehow that seemed to get across.

"We had another lunch. Then I felt bold enough to ask their opinion. They said, 'This lunch hour is not enough. Could we have evening suppers so that we can spread ourselves?' More and more of the two sections came. Soon they were arriving at 6.00 and not leaving till 11 p.m. In the next nine months there were in all twelve such occasions.

"One can only say that seed thoughts have been planted in men's minds. When those people meet again in conference situations they will not be strangers but people who know each other as persons. This friend of mine, the African lecturer with whom I planned it all, said, 'Strangely enough I have never even seen my own colleagues in this relaxed frame of mind.'

"From all this one point is clear. For God-guided purposes should each of us not first look at our own sphere of influence? A few people starting where they are could take this spirit so that it penetrates and infuses our society."

The Professor and his wife point to other bridge-building initiatives which they know of and appreciate. They feel they have done nothing remarkable.

At a time when matters of life and death for a whole country hang on decisions and relationships at a conference table, who knows?

5. A SOWETO STORY

Soweto is a hard school. The viciousness of the riots in that sprawling, teeming city of a million blacks just outside Johannesburg drives the point home. Naked feelings stood revealed. In those surroundings you do not become a leader of community projects without learning the facts of life.

One glance at June Chabaku and you know she has her feet firmly planted on the ground. There is an immovable look about her, but also a twinkle of humour in her eye. When she says that she held the Transvaal high jump record for nine years, she chuckles, "You wouldn't think it to see me now."

If you came into a room and heard that deep, resonant voice, you would, like as not, look around for a large, powerful man. But then June is surprising in many ways.

She leapt into prominence nationally in 1975 during International Women's Year, when she was elected to the Chair of the IWY Transvaal Committee, representing leading women of all races. She appeared several times on national television and often in the press. Her speech to the International Convention of a thousand women in Grahamstown brought both radicals and conservatives to their feet in an ovation. For many whites it was a shock to hear a black woman from an unsophisticated background speak with such authority. It awoke a totally new respect. "I admire her. She is so dynamic", said one Afrikaner who only the day before had threatened to walk out because of politics.

June is certainly no creampuff or pushover for anyone. From her earliest days she showed her determination. She was one of seven children. Her father was a clerk, her mother a simple woman who thought a girl's place was in the kitchen and reading a waste of time. That did not deter June. She picked up discarded pens and exercise books. The pens she cleaned and sharpened; the unused sheets of paper she glued together and recovered. Then she sold them to earn her school fees. Her father saw her spirit and backed her. He brought newspapers home which awoke her interest in the outside world. She passed her Junior Certificate and then, while teaching, took her Matric.

Politics soon began to touch her. Perhaps her first shock came when her father, a deeply religious man, resigned from his church because racialism had come into the Sacraments – one chalice for whites, another for blacks.

Education was a very sensitive subject. The majority of the blacks looked on the introduction of the new Bantu Education Act as an attempt to impose an inferior quality on them. June and other teachers pulled out and started a private school, but although their results were good, this was closed. The black boycott was finally broken and 97% were forced by economic circumstances to resume teaching.

But not June. Her bitterness fanned into a flame. She lived for three years on odd jobs, selling newspapers and insurance. Then she became fulltime organiser of the Women's League of the African National Congress. When this was banned, she returned once more to teaching.

At this point something new hit her. It happened through Philip Vundla, militant leader of the Transvaal blacks, a man whose whole background was strikes and boycotts. He said that he had found a new weapon in his battle for change, which altered his whole approach.*

* See *P.Q. The Story of Philip Vundla of South Africa*, by Kathleen Vundla.

June tells the story: "We young people yearned and longed for the type of leadership that Mr. Vundla gave us. To him there was no watery middle of the road. Things were black or white, not grey, red or white, not pink. When he took up this new idea we did not understand. We called him a renegade. We felt he had diverted from the national course.

"We thought the only way to deal with anybody we disagreed with was to get rid of him, so we assaulted him. It was at night in a Board Room of the Advisory Council. We used knives, stones and sticks. He managed to escape through a window, badly wounded and landed in hospital.

"We knew that he knew who had assaulted him. The thing that got me was that even as he lay there swollen up with pangs of pain, the bruises and the blows we had rained on him, he said, 'I will not lay a charge against these people. I have a new idea. I know what causes them to do that.' That struck me. I wondered how many of us would have such guts, how many of us can actually forgive when somebody has hurt us and wounded us, so that we can still love that person and forgive in our hearts.

"That was what made me feel there must be something in this man to risk his life for something greater than his life. That is what attracted me."

Unexpectedly June laughs. "Basically women are regarded as very soft, sweet and gentle, apologetic and willing to work. But this approach was not for me. I have always been a rebel. In that spirit I found this idea that Mr. Vundla had and began to try it in my own life."

Then came a big step forward for June. She got an offer to study drama in London. It was from a group involved in the theatre of the black people. They offered to pay for her lodging and part of her school fees. She was grateful for this. On her way she decided to go via the Moral Re-Armament conference at Caux in Switzerland. Her friends helped her raise the extra money to do this.

When she got to London a little later than scheduled, though still in time for the school opening, some people got to know that she had been to Caux. They objected and withdrew the £500 which was to pay for her lodging and fees.

"You can imagine what it is like to be in a strange land," she goes on, "when you know nobody and you have the landlady saying, 'The week is past, I need my money.' And you are black in a white area and the school needs the money too."

Even remembering this years later brings tears to June's eyes. "So many people came to me, offering to be at my disposal. They told me, 'Look, you can come and be on our platform. Tell them what apartheid is. Speak about the unjust laws in your country. You'll have bursaries, you'll have everyone helping you in your studies.' I refused. Certainly these things they spoke of are wrong, but I was not going to be used by anyone. I was going to fight these things as I thought right. I was going to be my own master."

She becomes reminiscent again. During the lunch time, when the students went to the canteen for their meal, she would go down to the lake and sit there because she could not afford to have a meal. She was convinced that what she stood for was bigger than a meal.

For two and a half months June would not write to her family, not wanting to worry them. "Those people used to follow me. They would say, 'Stop your fight. Forget these ideas of yours.' But I knew that I had to pay the price." Then a lady in Johannesburg sold part of her belongings so that June could pay her fees.

June pauses thoughtfully. These things had caused her a great deal of hurt. "But I was learning," she said, "that when God has a purpose, He will put you on an anvil and hammer you so that you become tough and able to do what He wants. At the time you may not realise what the purpose is."

June shone at college, gaining her diplomas in drama, teaching and in theatre production in only one year. But when she returned to South Africa the Bantu Education Department rejected her qualifications. "It broke my heart," she said, "and I decided again to leave teaching."

She became a community services youth club leader with the Johannesburg City Council. In Soweto they still talk of a meeting which June organised when the leaders of thirteen notorious gangs brought all their members together to pledge that they would disband. The clubs grew enormously but, later, June felt that whites with little experience and no feel for the community were appointed above her. Once more she resigned in protest. She then spent time touring the country organising literary and training courses.

June knows well that change will not happen cheaply. Again she talks from experience. At African National Congress meetings she was always a dynamic speaker. She would often speak at the end because her colleagues knew that she could express their vision with force, fire and determination.

"At the same time," she says, "I had come to hate my mother because I felt she was taking advantage of my father. This cancer of hate robbed me of the cleansing fire so that I could not fight with clean hands. This is the kind of thing that breaks so many of us in our families.

"How many of us fight with our in-laws? How many of us don't get on with sisters or brothers? It is not just black and white that divide. We may make big speeches about unity among our own people, but then someone says, 'How can you believe him when he has left this or that kind of dirt behind in his own family?' This often robs us of the dynamic leadership we need."

She refers back to Philip Vundla. "We thought at first that he would become soft. But no! He became stronger because he was clear in himself, and wanted nothing for himself."

Her eyes sparkle and her voice takes on extra resonance. "We have to become people who, when a thing is wrong, say it is wrong without fear because we want nothing for ourselves."

June spoke in these terms to several hundred tough trade union leaders, most of them white, at the annual Trade Union Congress of South Africa in Cape Town in 1975. She talked of the simple, human problems of being black in their society. She did not point the finger, but she challenged them to lead a movement for justice and equality throughout the country. Some months later a friend was talking to a white official of the Rhodesian Railway Workers. "If you can get that woman to come here I will round up everyone in the place to hear her," he said.

"I have to ask myself, 'how effective can I be in my fight?' " June continues. "Coming from South Africa and accepting to be used by God does not mean that I say that everything there is wonderful. Oh no! I am still voteless. I am still voiceless. I am still landless. There is a lot we have to put right.

"But hate is not the most effective way. So many of us hate each other because of our positions, because you oppose me. This makes us the slave of those we hate. They colour all we do.

44

No! The very person you hate is the person you have got to win. Otherwise he undercuts everything you do."

She appeals to the white man with all her heart. "It is now time to sacrifice. You say to yourselves in your fear, 'If we give one finger they will take the whole hand,' while the blacks say, 'Why should we give a finger when they have been having the whole body for generations?' It cuts both ways.

She emphasises what Vundla and Nkomo stood for. "We need leaders today who will not be bought by selfish, personal ambition so that they lose their goal and become concerned with entrenching themselves where they are. This is true of leaders throughout the world, whether black, white or yellow. When you meet some white cabinet ministers as individuals they burn with goodwill, they yearn for a change, they would love to see things different. But have they the guts to stand for that? They fear their electorate, thinking, 'What will I lose?' "

June, however, does not take the easy road of just blaming others. "I cannot ask for honesty from the Government," she says, "when I am not honest. I cannot ask for people to be un-selfish when I just think of my own interests."

She tells a vivid story. "There was a woman who hated me because I took up the challenge of fighting with clean hands. One day she met me on the train. Her venom was so strong that she spat on me. I had to get off at the next station to avoid all the passengers hearing her outburst. Later I heard that she was divorced and could not get a house. She had two children. I prayed that God would give me a chance so that, in her hour of need, I could be there to help her. I was able to put her on my lodger's permit, and then made sure that she could get accommodation, that the children could go to school, and that her reference books were put in order. She was astounded that

45

I rather than her personal friends was the one who could come and assist her.

"This I have learnt. If someone takes a brick and throws it at you to kill you, take that brick and build a home for him. You will leave him with a pricked conscience for life. He will never forget you.

"I say to you what has been said to me:

Dare to be a Daniel,
Dare to stand alone;

Dare to have a purpose true,
Dare to make it known."

6. NO IVORY TOWER

Cornelius Marivate has been close to the eye of the hurricane in the recent Transvaal disturbances. He is a lecturer in Bantu Languages at the University of South Africa and has been active in the School Boards in his township of Attridgeville, just outside Pretoria.

Students for whose education he is responsible have clashed head on with the police. Young men whom he knows have been shot. Every weekend high school boys come to him for advice. He is no ivory tower academic.

He describes what he sees around him. "Extreme blacks who say, 'Away with the whites! We will never get redress. We must rely on ourselves alone.' Whites who say, 'We must have a bigger and stronger defence force;' who think of clustering more and more into a corner. Yet white security must, in the final analysis, depend on the goodwill of the blacks, rather than on fear and shooting. While for us blacks it is moonshine to think we can chase four million whites into the sea. Their 'knowhow' is needed and this country is their home too. It is only when we come into the open and hide nothing and want only the best that we will be able to build a good South Africa.

"Above all," says Marivate, "We need maturity. We are bogged down in the mud of colour. We need the maturity to lift ourselves above our own group and what they think; the maturity to think further than the identity of black or white; the maturity to talk in terms of human beings in South Africa. This maturity is like a fruit. When a fruit is ripe it cannot cling to the tree or it is of no use. It must be detached. A man, if he is mature, must detach himself and become independent in his spirit. You can only get that if you come to depend on a new authority. Perhaps it is the authority drawn from silence. In silence a man can get his own independent inspiration so that he dares to do what is right."

Marivate talks from what he has been through himself. He himself has clashed with white authority.

In Attridgeville he was a member of the School Board of which the late Dr. William Nkomo was Chairman. An official of the Education Department, much against the wishes of the people, pushed through a division of the Board into ethnic units, each responsible for its own section of schools. Marivate's people were very bitter about this. Especially in the towns they felt that this was done to weaken their bargaining power.

The official, however, was adamant and the plan went through. Marivate concluded that there was little they could do. For the sake of the children they had to participate.

The individual chairmen of the sub-divided Boards regrouped, however, and came together to form a committee to produce a memorandum protesting against the compulsory use of Afrikaans. At the end of 1974 another big issue arose. About 750 children could not find accommodation in existing high schools. The same official was against building another school. He said that many of the children should rather re-sit their previous year's exams. Marivate and his colleagues disagreed. The 'memorandum committee' was given a mandate to create a new school for these children and Marivate was appointed Chairman.

"We went straight away to the Department of Education," he remarks. "The senior man was helpful. It was agreed we should establish the school. Teachers were to be temporarily seconded from existing schools. The school was registered."

At this point the earlier official, who had been away on leave, returned. He found himself having to deal with the same men – and Marivate in particular – who had opposed his previous plans. He said he would have nothing to do with them. The committee must be completely re-constituted.

Marivate refused. With the parents' backing, he and his colleagues decided to raise funds to continue independently.

The official was furious. He telephoned Marivate. "Do you think you are the new Regional Director, giving counter-instructions to mine?" he burst out.

"Can I come and see you?" replied Marivate.

"No! I have no time."

At this point Marivate remembered that this man's father had died a few days previously. "Please accept my heartfelt sympathy," he said.

There was a pause. Then the official said, "Come and see me on Wednesday."

The previous day the thought had crossed Marivate's mind, "The bitterness you have towards this man is very costly to the people you serve." When the Wednesday came Marivate went to the Department. The official was standing ready to leave. "Well, what is it?" he asked. "I have no time."

Marivate said, "I try to listen to God. I have come to apologise for my personal bitterness against you. It is not manly. I cannot work with you like that."

The official stood silent for a moment. Then he said, "Sit down. Yes, I have felt this all the time. I accept what you say." He said he, too, was sorry for the way he had acted and that, perhaps, this also had been the cause of the trouble. "I did not want to work with you people," he added. He had, he said, just been drawing up names for the new committee Board. "Would you mind to serve on it?" he asked.

Marivate said he would think about it. The official said, "Please. After all, you are the man who has started the school. I have not wanted to work with you, but now we can work together."

Marivate agreed to serve and is now Vice-Chairman.

The official then told him that he had been about to refuse grants for the new school. Now, however, he was going to recommend them. "I have them here in my pocket," he said, and pulled them out.

"We had been prepared to go it alone," says Marivate, "but instead of having to make the parents sacrifice, the teachers' salaries now came straight away from the Department."

A real friendship, man to man, grew up between Marivate and the official. The latter supported the building of the school, where previously he had rejected it. What is more, he asked Marivate, "What do you think the needs are? You know, because you have been working on it." Marivate said that they did not just want the usual departmental plans. They investigated some new prototypes and, with the official's backing, built a school which Marivate proudly believes to be the best in Pretoria.

Marivate's readiness to take the first difficult step with the official had sprung from another incident several years earlier. At that time he was a district secretary/treasurer of the Transvaal United African Teachers' Association, responsible for thirteen branches. Often he had to speak out against dishonesty in some of the branch secretaries.

One day a friend faced him with the idea that, if he wanted people to be honest, he needed first to be honest with himself.

"I realised," he said, "that I myself had been misusing the funds. Over seven years I had taken R240."

Marivate decided to put this right. He had just reached the end of his term of service, but he wrote to his committee telling them what he had done and that he would refund the money. "My pride and my fear of losing the esteem of the others made that the hardest letter I had ever written. I was sure they would say, 'Just look at this man who has talked so glibly about honesty.' "

For two months he heard nothing from the committee. A few tentative enquiries were brushed aside. Then he received an invitation from the executive to a farewell function to mark the end of his service. "Ah," he thought, "They are keeping it all to get at me there."

The day came and he went along with the money in his pocket. When he spoke he told them again what he had done and produced the R240. "No," they said, "We have decided that this R240 is to be your farewell present!"

Instead of accusing him the other branch secretaries wanted to know what had made him to be so honest. After all, the auditors had passed the books and there had been no sign that any money was missing. Some of those who asked took a fresh look at themselves.

"These kind of things can shut you in if they are not put right," Marivate says today. "You are not free to be the man you are meant to be. You become a prisoner of the things you have done wrong, just as you can become a prisoner of reaction to what others do wrong. We must be able to deal straight, man to man, because we are straight ourselves. It depends on our decisions.

"We can create our own framework of freedom with everyone we meet."

7. THE PLATTELANDERS

Who controls? Who has the final say? This is perhaps *the* question in Southern Africa – or indeed in a hundred other countries.

Here in South Africa I know sincere white men and sincere black men who see their interests as entirely at odds. I have talked to black men who are not interested in making any part of the present system work because it has been conceived, without consultation, by whites. I have talked to white men who are certain they would be cutting their own throats if they gave away any part of the right of decision. So where do you go from there?

If the choice remains *your* control or *my* control, deadlock seems inevitable. We are back to the law of the jungle. For any man who calls himself a Christian there should be a third alternative – God-control.

That may seem altogether too simplistic a solution when one thinks of the enormity of problems and pressures. But is it worth trying? What if it has already been tried?

Three rather unexpected men may indicate something of what can happen. All three are white farmers. When people discuss South Africa you often hear it said, "Oh, it may be possible for change to come among the intellectuals or even the businessmen. But as for the farmers on the platteland* . . ."

* the country districts.

It takes six hours driving from Pretoria to reach Piet Naude's farm. You head North East across the open high veld, then suddenly begin to drop down the escarpment through rugged valleys into the bush veld where thorn trees shut you in. It is hot. You go on till you are almost at the vast Kruger National Park. Beyond that is the Mozambique border.

Piet and his neighbours are comparative new comers to the area, for only the development of irrigation schemes has made the land fertile, growing fruit and vegetables for the distant cities.

Piet is of Huguenot origin and he and his wife count themselves as true Boer stock. Piet's forbears trekked on and on in search of land they could call their own. Mrs. Naude's grandfather was in Paul Kruger's government of the old Transvaal Republic. Her great uncle, as Secretary General of the Republic, had the unhappy task of handing over control to the British, following the exile of President Kruger.

As you sit on his stoep with the sounds of the bush all around you, 'Oom Piet's' talk roams widely over the country. He speaks of unexpected people whom he counts as friends – black nationalists in Rhodesia, Homeland Chief Ministers and overseas politicians. For he finds himself working out new patterns of relationships between black and white, boss and worker, which interest many. I heard a black Chief Minister say of him, "Multiply Piet Naude and you have an answer for South Africa."

Piet's upbringing gave him traditional attitudes. He says, "I suppose it was because of circumstances, but there was a very big division between black and white. We brought the Gospel to the black people but we never thought about relationships. In our home each evening my father would read from the Bible and the kitchen workers would come and sit and also listen. But that was all. I grew up with that feeling of absolute division. I tried to be kind. But I never thought their need might be greater than that."

Piet told of one experience which went right to his heart. The workers on the farm started getting sick. None of them came to work. It was a kind of bad 'flu. Piet asked, "What is happening? Will they get well? Will they come to work again?" He could get no answer from them.

He went to their homes and took them medicine, but they did not get better. "One day," he said, "I met one of the women. She could only walk with a stick. I said to her, 'Why don't you go to the house and get some medicine?' She said she could not walk that far.

"I came home and my heart felt raw," Piet says. "I wondered what to do. Then I thought 'Get some meat, cook it well, and send the strong soup to their houses.' So I did that, day after day. Within a few weeks they were all back on their feet. It's funny, but that is when I began to think of them as real people."

Piet paused a bit and then went back to the beginning. Everything had been going wrong on the farm. He tried everything, pointing the finger and threatening. But nothing succeeded. He and his wife had just about decided to throw in the towel.

Then he happened to go to a weekend gathering where he heard Cornelius Marivate tell of his decision to post the letter being honest about the money he had taken. Piet was shaken. He started to think, "If only I was as lucky as you. If only I could post my life away. But I can't."

He continued, "That evening in my room I took a little note-book and sat down and said, 'Lord, I know you can speak to people. Won't you please speak to me. Tell me what is wrong in my life.' The thought came to me and I wrote it down, 'You are frightened.' I said, 'But all people are frightened. What does this mean?'

"Then I wrote down, 'You are frightened in the first place in case your wife should find out about you; you are frightened in the second place that your neighbours will find out about you; you are frightened in the third place of giving your life to God in case you fall back again.'

"Then I closed the book. I said to God, 'I will never follow You. I can't. And I won't. But still I want to ask You one thing, and that is never to let go of me!' At that moment something happened in my heart and I knew I would never be the same again."

Next evening Piet went to visit some old friends. They said to him, "Piet, what about the usual – a coke with a double brandy?" Piet found himself saying, "No, thank you." They said, "What's wrong? Come on, you always have it." Again he said, No, thank you."

They went in to the table. It was a lovely meal. They said to Piet, "You surely are going to have a light table wine with us." Piet says, "I found myself saying, 'No, thank you.' But I didn't know what was going on inside me. They said, 'But listen, man, there must be something wrong!' All I could say was, 'No, thank you.' All of a sudden a big happiness came into my heart because I did not have to worry any more what people thought of me. 'You have been obedient in such a small thing,' the inner voice said, 'I will set you free in bigger things.' "

"One evening, a few days later, I was reading my Bible with

my wife. I came to the story of David, where he had the other man killed so he could take his wife. I said to the Lord, 'But why did You let me read this? David was an absolutely bad man!' The Lord said, 'Because I am showing you your life.'

"Then I saw that I had done everything that David had done except to let the other man be killed. The Lord said, 'Tonight you will become absolutely honest with your wife.'

"I said, 'Never! Never! Never! We are happy now. We have beautiful children and grandchildren and this will definitely mean a divorce. I can't do it. I can't!'

"The Lord said, 'This is your valley of death. I will be with you.'

"I started to tell my wife everything, right through to the marrow. It was like a two-edged sword. Then there was a long silence. I knew my wife was going to say, 'I've often told you you were doing those things and you have always denied it.' Then she said, 'My husband, I will forgive you. And I will forget.' You know, people often say, 'I will forgive.' But they are not willing to forget. That meant a whole new start in our lives.

"I have found now that when I am fullhearted, then the strength is there. But if I am half-hearted, wanting to hold something back, then it is a struggle."

Piet went on to tell what happened on the farm. "This is how it began," he said. "God asked me one day, 'What about your workers?' I said, 'Lord, that I can't do. How will I be able to help them? I don't know their language. No! The missionaries can do it. I can't.'

"Things were not going well. When I gave them jobs to do, they would throw down their hoes and say, 'Too plenty work.' So one day, in desperation, I decided to ask God again.

"He said, 'You don't care for these people. You think only of your money and your purse.'

"Next morning when I arrived at work I said, 'Good morning! Good morning! Good morning!' They looked at me. What's happening with the white man now?

" I started to apologise for my behaviour and to work in a new spirit towards them. But the core of the change actually happened soon after. I was over at my neighbour's farm one day. They told me of one of their workers who had just lost his child, who was very dear to him.

"I thought, 'Go and talk to that man.' At first again I said, 'I can't.' However, I took my car and went to his place. I said to him, 'James, come and sit with me.' I sympathised with him. 'Yes,' he said, 'I want to kill myself and be united with my child.'

"Then, quite clearly, I thought, 'Tell him the deepest things in your life.' That was very hard for me. I had never thought of talking to a black man like that. But when I did it he really opened his heart to me and he, too, decided to give his life to God. It made such a difference to him. You cannot imagine the change.

"We started to work together. We had big meetings. At times we had hundreds of Africans coming. It was difficult to find buildings big enough. Many, many made decisions. It is so wonderful to bring some kind of creation in people and see the growth in them. This man himself learnt to read and write. He went to a Bible School in Pretoria and now, having finished his training, is giving evening classes to teach others what he has learned.

"I never go out of my room in the morning now without being prepared to reach deep into those I will be meeting, black or white. I don't always succeed. Often I am the biggest failure. Many times on the road I stop to give a man a lift. I know I have to be ready for each man. I can tell you that if roads and trees could talk, they could tell stories of new life coming to people."

Not everyone, of course, shouts "hallelujah" at what Piet does. Some of his white neighbours raise their eyebrows. But many who opposed his new attitude are now working with him.

Within his church it is the same. He is an Elder, but his directness shocked some. He tells story after story, however, of changes coming to dominees, professors and missionaries.

At a big conference in Pretoria, with four hundred people of all races present, one of the highlights was when Piet and his wife and six of his workers took the platform. His workers told in their own language of the way they had been cured of drugs, drunkenness, thieving and broken family lives. Most had never been in a big city before, much less stood before a great audience of black and white. But they spoke with certainty and dignity, and nodded their heads when Piet told of his own change.

You meet the outreach of Piet in unexpected places. Recently I was in Rhodesia. A leading Indian businessman there had become a friend of Piet's. Last year Piet dropped in unannounced. The businessman said, "If this is not the guidance of God, I don't know what is. Come in. I have just been telling two friends about you. Come and speak for yourself."

Piet found himself sitting down with two ANC black nationalists, one of whom had recently been in detention. When Piet launched into his story, they listened fascinated. They knew only too well what Piet represented.

All of a sudden Piet suggested they be silent for a few moments and see what God had to say. After a while one of the men said, "I was willing to kill white people, but now I want a new way. We want to keep in contact to learn to build instead of killing." Piet, later, had a number of letters from one of them. He said, "Something happened in that office that morning to those two men and to me. And to my Indian friend as well."

I was with Piet a short time after the desperate riots in Johannesburg and Cape Town. Like many he had been deeply churned up inside. He said he felt like hating the rioters. All sorts of old instinctive reactions reared their heads.

He said, "I asked God, 'Please tell me what the cause of those riots is.' He said to me, and I wrote it down, 'Your actions as whites, the way you behave, is one of the causes!'

" 'You have not had the sympathy and the care for those of other colours.

" 'You have not succeeded in winning their love, their trust or their appreciation.

" 'Fundamentally you did discriminate and make them feel small, and they grew up without respect for you. The climate that you have built was not healthy. You have taught them the Bible but have often lived the opposite. Through the years bitterness grew in their hearts and they told it to their children and it was planted in their children's hearts.

" 'They are less privileged and it was your duty to build them. You have bossed them. They saw that as suppression.'

"It is not yet too late," Piet says. "We can still see our mistakes and put them right. We can come with true repentance and ask forgiveness and help to be different. Perhaps this is the thing Prime Minister Vorster is seeing and trying to bring to the people. If we put our mistakes right, the Lord is true to forgive us and help us bring about the right."

To a stranger the very idea seems extraordinary. Farm such land? Impossible! Yet Roly Kingwill has been doing just that on 27 000 acres, six thousand feet up in the Sneeuberg mountains of the Karoo.

The Karoo looks like a vast, unending stretch of semi-desert. It is bigger than Ireland. The harsh, stony soil grows only wiry, heatherlike bushes interspersed with tough tufts of sour grass. In winter the nights freeze hard and mountain farms carry extra stores to keep them going if the snows isolate them. The daytime sun dries up any faint moisture. In summer it is burning hot and one prays, often more in faith than hope, for the occasional thunderstorm to bring relief.

In the past couple of years there have been extraordinarily good rains, coming early enough in the summer and softly enough to soak into the hardbaked soil and allow fresh growth, so the dams and underground springs are replenished. Previously there had been years of vicious droughts, when what rains there were did not come till the end of summer and then exploded, battering the ironhard ground and running off before much of the water could be absorbed. Within a few weeks the frosts would come and growth would stop.

When, early this century, Roly Kingwill's father trekked the fifty miles into the mountains, climbing three thousand feet from Graaff Reinet, South Africa's fourth oldest town, much of the journey was by the roughest of tracks. As they went higher and higher the old African, who was driving the ox-wagon with all the household goods on board, finally burst out, "Why do you want to build a farm up here where even a baboon would need a stick to walk?"

But the Kingwill father had a will to match the toughness of his surroundings. He imported shorthorn cattle from overseas and began to rear pure-bred merino sheep. He surrounded the farm with many kilometres of jackal-proof wire fence. He built a magnificent homestead and named it Gordonville, after General Gordon of the Sudan.

It was always a struggle. When his father retired and Roly took over, a neighbour said to him, "You are fools to come here. The Sneeuberg are finished."

Kingwill tells it from his own angle. "Despite hardships I actually grew up among the privileged of South Africa. I could get a good education, go to university, and even travel abroad." But coming from a lonely farm where, in the early days, there was no 'phone and no car, he was a shy and reserved boy. "Very raw," he describes himself. It was difficult for him even to give his name to strangers, he was so embarrassed. But he was ambitious and trained hard and played a lot of rugby and cricket.

One day, back at home, he got an infected hand. He went into Graaff Reinet to see the doctor, met the doctor's daughter, and before long they were married. With the help of a full bond from the bank he negotiated for a farm of his own and began family life.

Through the depression of the thirties they had no money at all. A bad drought cost them many sheep. But they hung on. When you meet Kingwill and see that solid build and those blue eyes which seem to look away out to the mountains, you sense a man who lives into the pace of the seasons, rather than in the frenetic struggle for what today alone brings.

He needed all his patience. Short booms when wool prices rocketed up alternated with long slumps. I have stayed with them in mid-winter and seen how the lighting of a fire in the sitting-room was a decision never taken lightly. An extra jersey was more economical.

Today, Kingwill has become an outstanding leader in his community. On June 23rd, 1975, the *Graaff Reinet Advertiser* wrote, "On Saturday night Mr. Roland Kingwill of Gordonville became the first recipient of an award for outstanding services rendered to his community. The award was made by the Rotary Club of Graaff Reinet and is presented to an individual who is not a Rotarian but who gives 'Service before Self', the basic motto of Rotary International".

The paper went on, "We can think of nobody worthier of being honoured in this way. Mr. Kingwill moves quietly in many spheres of community life and especially champions the cause of those who do not enjoy the same privileges he does".

The paper referred to "the modern, comfortable homes" he had built for his staff at Gordonville, and concluded, "He always speaks with wisdom and deliberate thought on a host of matters and always has an attentive audience because of the sincerity with which he pleads a cause. He must indeed be a happy man that his wife and their family have followed in his footsteps and have had the courage to say what must be said without fear or favour or prejudice. On behalf of this community we congratulate him on this award which is so justly deserved."

It was not always so. When he first began to step out from convention and to take a different road, more mocked than honoured him.

Various things had made him begin to question what his life added up to. Was it enough just to farm to get a living, while making the weekends as long and enjoyable as possible? His children were growing, but his eldest daughter seemed shy of him. What would the future hold for them? And for the country? There were the divisions between Afrikaans and English, black and white; there was the disastrous spread of soil erosion all around him, with 400 000 000 tons of topsoil draining away the lifeblood of the land each year.

As he thought about these things he happened to read a book about the possibility of God actually controlling what you do. That made him pause. Then he met a young couple who said they had tried it. "I saw in them a freedom, a joy and a purpose in life which I coveted," he says.

Yet he doubted the reality of God. He was full of fear. He hesitated long. Finally he decided there was nothing to lose. One evening, as a shy, inferior-feeling and isolated young farmer, he sat alone in front of the fire. He said to God, "If you can speak, speak to me now." Clear as a bell, the answer seemed to come, "I have work for you." Then, like Piet Naude, he knew he needed to be absolutely honest with his wife, Moira, about things in the past which he had never told any-one.

It was not easy, but a new freedom and lightness of heart came to him. He found to his surprise that Moira had been thinking along the same lines. There were other resentments and dishonesties to be put right. He began to find what it was to live without pretence.

As these things were cleared up wider horizons began to open up. "I had to go to our Afrikaans neighbours to seek a new relationship and to admit where we had been wrong and superior in our attitudes," he says. He learnt to speak fluent Afrikaans.

Up till this time Kingwill had never been a member and seldom attended meetings of the Farmers' Association. He began to take an active part. It was a totally new experience for him to speak up in debates. Soon he was District Secretary and within a few years, Chairman. Later he was to become Mayor of New Bethesda, the nearest town.

Soil erosion was beginning to worry people. Kingwill at first thought of big national conservation schemes. "But," he says, "I felt that God was telling me to start on my own farm." He had bought the farm on the basis of running one sheep to two morgen (four acres). He had a full bond on the assumption that 3 000 sheep would bring in 30 000 lbs of wool a year. He was still suffering from the depression. "But I felt quite clearly that the heart was being eaten out of my land and that I should cut down my stock by one third," he says. "I had only been thinking of what I could make for myself."

Such a cut seemed a crazy idea. It would mean an immediate loss of income and real hardship. But he reduced his flock from 3 500 to 2 400. He introduced rotational grazing schemes and began to build dams to conserve water. Slowly results appeared. First the grass and veld cover began to increase. Then he noticed that the sheep were growing more wool per animal and the percentage of lambing was going up. Within five years it was clear that it had been a right step from every angle.

Others noticed the difference. He was asked to be in the lead of the anti-soil erosion campaign which was launched nationally. Later Government-sponsored experiments proved that his new stocking rate was scientifically right for the area. During the drought crisis of the 1960s the Government subsidised farmers who followed the example which Kingwill had made, sacrificially, on his own initiative.

He was also a pioneer of other technical advances in veld management. With his sons he was able to double the number of cattle they ran. Many mistakes were made, but steadily the graph rose. Good grass covered the once bare ground and the soil was anchored in position.

Then Kingwill began to think about his black workers. "We had alternated between appeasement and terrific rows," he says. "I had begun the daily practice of listening to God, even though as a farmer it meant getting up at 5.00 a.m. to have undisturbed time. One morning I thought, "Apologise to the staff for your outbursts of temper and tell them you are starting on a new basis".

He thought this was suicidal. Imagine how people would laugh if they heard of a white man acting like this with his black servants. He hesitated for some days. Then, early one morning, he called them together. To his surprise none of them took advantage or treated him with disrespect. A new understanding and trust began to grow.

Other things followed. He improved wages and provided healthier nourishment. He built them better houses with glass windows. The neighbours did make fun of this, but now all the workers' houses in the neighbourhood have glass windows.

An even more unusual step was to build a school on the farm. This roused more mockery. Fear of people getting "uppity", as the Americans would say, went the rounds. But Kingwill appointed a teacher and went ahead. "Today," he says, "our workers can keep the books and take much more responsibility. Their interest in the job has increased. They join us when we make plans for the farm and this is a further step in their education. Now it is national policy to have such farm schools and the Government pays the teachers' salaries."

In all these developments his wife, Moira, was an equal partner and often the clear interpreter of what was right on the farm and in the home.

Kingwill knows that everyone needs a feeling of security. One day he told the workers they could regard the farm as their home as long as they were prepared to take responsibility for it. He would not send them away or fire them when times were hard. Since then the workers have steadily improved their own standard of living, and drunkenness, for example, is no longer a problem.

Kingwill's experience of change in his own life is something he is ready to pass on to anyone at any time. It is on this base that all else is built. It has meant care replacing fear. And, as time has passed, he has discovered that much more is needed than just seeing what he could do for the black man. He got to know outstanding Africans such as Philip Vundla and found that he had much to learn from such men.

"In fact," he says, "It is essential for a white South African to get to know such men and discover what *they* really feel and what *they* think needs to happen. We need to learn more about ourselves through looking through their eyes."

Of course, on the farm, it has not all been sweetness and light. Kingwill's two sons, David and Robert, have been working the farm with him and have increasingly taken over responsibility. Each is married with small children; each of the three men – and the three wives – is a character, craggy as the kopjes among which they live. Clash is normal, and resentments and reactions have to be dealt with, as in any family.

Shortly after the city riots had shaken South Africa one of the daughters-in-law said, "I realise how my own family has got caught in the cross-fire of my feelings." She was honest and said she was sorry for the cost of this. Her new freedom had a big part in new initiative by the whole family in the community. With the two young wives in the lead, they arranged a meeting at which members of the Town Council together with black, brown, English and Afrikaner headmasters and churchmen discussed a programme of "bridge building" for the community.

It was a stormy occasion. But out of it came many more meetings and opportunities for honest exchange and practical planning. And history was made in Graaff Reinet when, a few months later, the town's inter-racial leadership was invited to a civic reception in the Town Hall to meet West Indian cricketer, Conrad Hunte, who was visiting the Kingwills.

Roly Kingwill remarked, "It has been encouraging to see some of the senior men in the area move from hardline resistance to enthusiastic support for this kind of initiative."

The ideas worked out on the farm spread in other ways. The *Graaff Reinet Advertiser* of 16th July, 1976, reported on its front page a talk given by David Kingwill on the subject of farm labour at a Symposium attended by the Minister of Coloured Relations, farmers and officials. This same talk has since been given at a University of Cape Town conference.

David, who is Vice-Chairman of the Midlands Agricultural Union, said that he was speaking from the experience of change first begun by his father. "We still have a long way to go," he told the Symposium. "We do not claim to have all the answers, but we have seen the growth in character and understanding of a large number of farm workers and their families."

The *Advertiser* listed the following ten points from his talk:
1. Attitudes and habits of the boss are of great importance. Indisciplined, drunk or lazy bosses are not likely to motivate discipline and responsibility.

2. Men and women on the staff must know they are trusted with both goods and responsibilities and that their ideas are respected. Sometimes they have better ways of doing things than we do.

3. Social life is important. To cater for social opportunities. Use of farm sheds, loan of vehicles, lifts to town and shopping opportunities must be seen as part of what is due to them and necessary for happiness.

4. Spiritual and moral values matter. Like everyone else they need spiritual stimulation. They take church life seriously, if given the chance.

5. There must be a relationship which allows for discussion on problems that arise; wages, work hours, housing, sport etc. – as well as squabbles among the staff themselves. Opportunities for discussion should be created – and the boss can make mistakes!

6. Profit cannot be the only criterion. The men and women of the farm must be seen as assets to be built on – not problems to be solved.

7. A fair day's wage for a fair day's work – with adjustments for training, responsibility and loyalty. A sense of purpose and possibility of advancement.

8. Security is as important to the worker as it is to us. This goes for the man as well as his wife. They need to feel needed and useful. They cannot be expected to take pride in their homes – or in any aspect of the farm – unless they have the certainty they will be there tomorrow to benefit.

9. The wives are just as important as the men. The farm wife must be ready to give time and trouble to help them learn various housecrafts. Once learnt, they will teach others.

10. Food and clothing adequate for their needs must be available as well as educational opportunities for their children.

The correspondent of the Afrikaans farmers' paper *Landbou Weekblad* made these points his main story jointly with the Minister's speech. He said to Roly Kingwill, "Your thinking has been twenty years ahead of others." Kingwill replied, "It is because I got direction from God."

On December 24th 1976, *Landbou Weekblad* made the story of Gordonville its main feature, saying that what Roland, David and Robert Kingwill are working out "can serve as an example for many farmers".

Their writer, after three pages of story and photos, summed it up as "the revolution (omwenteling) which Roland Kingwill initiated, a revolution which can expand still further and whose final outcome cannot be foreseen.

IN MATABELELAND

When you first meet Basil Kew you would hardly think of him as likely to be a trusted friend of men who could decide Rhodesia's future. This weather-beaten, rather shy man, hesitant in speech and unassuming in manner, clearly lives close to the land.

He was born and brought up in the city life of Johannesburg, but always wanted to farm. He worked to gain some experience. Then, with £135 borrowed from his father, he negotiated under the contributory purchase scheme for 400 acres near Bulawayo in Rhodesia, and began on his own. Later he managed to add a further 200 acres, but by Rhodesian standards his has always been a small concern.

Slowly he built up a dairy herd, with some crops to supplement the cattle. It was just enough for him and his wife, Muriel to make a living and raise a family.

Conditions were tough and so was Basil. He had a fiery temper and often laid about him with his workers. After some time word went back along the grapevine to Nyasaland, from where many of the workers came, and Basil found himself blacklisted by the Africans. His supply of labour began to dry up.

The same thing happened to others. A neighbour called him up one day and said, "Basil, I'm finished. I've only got $1\frac{1}{2}$ men left, one man and a boy. I can't carry on. I'm selling up."

A great fear grew in Basil that the same thing was going to happen to him. He developed ulcers and the strain brought on haemorrages. One followed another. After the fourth, the doctor told him he was lucky to have survived and that something had got to change.

Just at that time a farming friend said to him, "Have you seen that play 'The Forgotten Factor' in town? It's good." Basil and Muriel decided to go. The play dramatised the idea that, in realms of conflict, men could find from God an unexpected factor. Basil was intrigued. He decided to see if it would work. He took a piece of paper and asked God to show him where to begin. To his horror the first thing he found himself writing down was, "Apologise to Peter".

Peter was a ten year old African boy whom he had thrashed. He was a rascal and deserved something, but Basil had lost his temper and beaten him till he had forced tears from the stubborn little boy. Basil tried to push the thought away. For days he kept saying it was stupid. But it gnawed away at him.

It happened that Basil had just got his first-ever new car,

a Morris Oxford. It was his pride and joy. He nursed it like a baby.

His inner turmoil about Peter, however, grew and grew until one day he was driving on the farm and went right over a large boulder in the middle of the road. It was sitting there, perfectly clear and noticeable, but Basil was so confused in himself that he did not see it. This shook him. He said to Muriel, "Look, I don't know what is going to happen but I must try this."

He went to look for the youngster – he had quite a search to find him – and said simply that he was sorry he had given him such a thrashing and had lost his temper. Basil says, "It wasn't that I felt really sorry at all. But, strangely, immediately I said it – and it was the hardest thing I ever did in my life – I actually was very sorry. It came home to me what I had done."

From that day Basil began to make friends with Africans. Things changed completely on the farm and his ulcers disappeared, never to return. He had always limited his friendship to his European neighbours. Now he became a wellknown figure in the black townships of Bulawayo. He got to know senior African leaders, men whose interests had never crossed his mind before. His concern became not just creating good relationships, but how black and white could build the quality of leadership the country would need.

He has become a man who is prepared to talk straight to anyone if he feels that there are things, however uncomfortable, which need to be said. This does not come easily to him. He only does it when pushed by a sense that it is God's will. Sometimes men react and hit back, only to appreciate later that Basil wants nothing except to see the highest qualities of leadership blossom in those he counts as friends.

At the end of 1976 the local African principal asked Basil to be guest of honour at his school prize-giving. He introduced him as one to whom they all owed much and who now thought not in terms of black and white, but in terms of men.

Basil works for relationships based on the solid rock of honesty and expecting the best of the other man. Such relationships are going to be sorely needed. Basil, himself, believes that the farms count for much. 90 % of the country's people depend on them. A hundred people live on his 600 acres alone. What is built there will be the country's future.

"HOLY JOE" AND THE MILITANTS

Howard Eybers has been in one of the hottest seats imaginable in South Africa. He was Chairman of the Student Representative Council of the coloured University of the Western Cape up to March 1976.

As one talks to the Western Cape students feelings boil to the surface. These reflect the bitterness at all the black universities. It is described in the official Snyman Report into the disturbances at the University of the North; seen in the burning of their own buildings by students at the University of Zululand, and in the closure of the University of Fort Hare. As I write Western Cape is also closed for a week as students protest their solidarity with their colleagues up north.

The Snyman Report makes it clear that, among students, general frustrations with the whole position in the country is something more than local grievances, more than the work of agitators.

In 1975 Howard put himself forward for election to the SRC. He stood as a committed Christian. To his surprise he was elected and then appointed Chairman. He was older than the average student so, perhaps, had added authority. He is a married man with two children. He had already worked for some years before deciding to study theology.

He comes from a background where, in many ways, things were against him. His father drank. As a child his home was a shack, his bed two hard, upright chairs put together. When it rained his job was to place the buckets to catch the drips through the roof. There were thirteen children and his mother died when he was seventeen. That same year three of his older brothers got married, so he was left with much of the family responsibility.

A third thing happened that year. Howard committed his life to God. He describes it as a right-about turn in his life. But his bitterness grew along with his faith. When one met him one sensed a divided spirit under that Afro haircut and the flowery phrases about Jesus and the love of God.

In January 1976 Howard was invited by Rev. Kanodereka and others to spend two weeks of his holidays in Rhodesia. He wanted to move out beyond South Africa's borders and see what they were doing up there, so he went. On arrival Kanodereka told him that he could have a part in healing rifts among the blacks in Rhodesia. "What, me?" he thought to himself. "There are so many rifts in my own life, and I don't even know these people."

He began to move around and meet young blacks and whites, militant leaders and student rebels. He stayed with a young white man called John. They went together to colleges and townships. John would tell people how a man like himself could change. He talked of absolute honesty, purity, unselfishness and love.

Howard says, "I was a real 'Holy Joe'. I was training for the ministry and I aimed to convert sinners wherever I went. But what John was saying got under my skin. This talk of those standards. He even suggested I might have a look at them myself. As though I needed that! Then he would get me up at 5.30 every morning, bringing me a cup of tea and suggesting that we should listen to God.

"I could see that all kinds of people were changing and that it was affecting the country," Howard says. "But, as the days went by, John made me more and more uncomfortable. Finally

I hit out viciously. 'You can keep all this talk of moral standards. I am a Christian. I don't need them.' I was very angry."

The next morning Howard got up and went to shave. "As I stood in the bathroom in front of the mirror," he goes on, "it was as though God suddenly grabbed me and shook me. For the first time I took a real, honest look at myself. I realised how much I was bluffiing.

"The first thought that came into my mind was, 'Your wife. You have been neglecting Rosetta and the children.' I was a guy who always wanted to boost my ego by being in the limelight. I was popular. I was always being invited to address clubs and preach and speak to the masses. How I enjoyed that! God said to me, 'You have been bluffing. You have said you wanted to serve Me, but you have been building yourself up while pretending to be humble.'

"The second thought I had was, 'Open your suitcase'. Now that may seem silly. But I opened the lid and there was a library book that was four years overdue. Oh, I had rationalised that it was just extended borrowing, but I knew, honestly, that it was more than that."

Howard returned home and put these things right. He started to be much more direct with people. "I had always wanted to please people," he says. "I did not speak out when things were wrong." He describes people like himself as "wearing rose-tinted glasses and a candyfloss front." A new clarity about purity helped. "I had always said to myself that it was just human to look at women. But I needed to be real about myself, then I could get clear of the dirt that kept me insecure and fearful."

Howard took his new ideas back with him to the campus. His fresh experience was so real to him that he thought others would quickly get the point. Some did. Others saw it as a threat to their bid for control and counterattacked sharply. It was a tough lesson in the ideological facts of life for which Howard was not yet fully prepared. He allowed himself to be pictured as a man whose platform was just mushy goodwill. In those surroundings, with that label, he hadn't a hope. He was pushed into a corner and finally resigned as Chairman.

He has learnt much since. In no sense has he retired hurt. It was he who invited Kanodereka and Smith to the campus. But he has seen that it is one thing to have a real, personal experience of Christ in your life. It is quite another to relate that realistically to the forces bidding for your nation.

A militant fellow-student of Howard's came to the 1975 Rhodesian conference. After some days he said to a friend, "I am not convinced by some of the people here. I am not convinced that their kind of 'change' will not soften me."

His friend thought over what the student had said. Then he went back to him. "For you," he told him, "The white man at this moment is irrelevant. The real issue for you is what sort of leadership your people deserve? What about the temptations of money, women, power or flattery? If you are not clear on these you will betray those you say you want to fight for."

The student chewed on this. Later he said, "That is true. I have been ready to climb over others to get where I am. I need to put this right."

One of the most able young coloured leaders said to me recently, "Any able man wants to get to the top. All of us know the attractions of personal power, financial security and the good opinion of others, but if any of these control me, then, however much I may say I want to fight the system, I become, in fact, a slave of the system."

The Howards of life have to tackle these questions constantly. What is the aim that goes beyond reconciliation? Could it be to set the militants free from the corruption, the fear, the bitterness or the greed that keeps their militancy limited? And to get the right sort of militancy into those who complain about others but do nothing themselves?

9. MAN OR BOY?

The big, suburban supermarket where Steven Sibare works is typical of a hundred others in Southern African cities. There is plenty of parking space for the cars of the well-to-do.

Steven is a cashier at one of the tills. As a young black man many things used to go through his mind as he dealt with the customers who flowed past. He compared their living conditions with his own, where he shared a hostel room with five others, and bathrooms and toilet with a hundred more. He counted himself lucky to have his present job, but seethed inside when he remembered how he was sacked from his previous work after a false accusation of stealing. He particularly blamed one white woman in that department. She had been very good to him, but after the accusation Steven, in his anger, thought she must have told stories about him. In revenge he spread lies about her.

Steven is one of the hundreds of young men in Salisbury who look to Rev. Kanodereka for leadership. When he heard him talk about how a man could be effective in changing first himself and then others Steven decided to experiment.

His first thought was to ask forgiveness from the white woman for the lies he had told, and to thank her for her care in the past. The blinkers of his bitterness lifted. He began to look at people with new eyes and with a new authority.

One day a customer came in and asked for a "boy" to take some empties from his car. Steven grinned at him and said, "I'm sorry, sir, we have no boys here. Would you like a man?" Taken aback, the man said, "Oh . . . yes". After he had got his refund on the bottles he came over to Steven again to ask him what he meant. "Well", said Steven, "African men work in the shop here, and African boys go to school".

"Before," went on Steven, "I had just burned inside when I was called 'boy'. Now I felt I could do something about it."

Another customer came in. "Could I have some cigarettes for my 'boy' please?" Steven asked, "How old is he?" "Oh, about forty, forty five." "Ah, well that is all right then," said Steven. "He is a man, for as far as I know boys are not allowed to smoke."

Steven laughs about it all. "I am so pleased because most of our chaps have taken up this idea. They refuse so cheerfully to be called 'boys'."

He had begun his campaign in the supermarket by writing a letter to each of his workmates, black and white, from the manager down, outlining what he was going to stand for. This was not easy for a junior employee to do. In his letter he said that they were all confronted with grave issues – bitterness, fear, injustice, arrogance. These things were inside their shop, their country, their homes and even in themselves. He told them that he had decided to change and that it was open for anyone to try. He ended by recommending them to read a book which had helped him make up his mind.

This aroused considerable controversy. Thirteen of his colleagues bought the book. One white despatch clerk asked indignantly why he had been sent the letter, saying that it was the terrorists who needed to change. Steven answered, "If you cannot change, the terrorists won't change. If you change, the terrorists can change".

At one stage the Head Office discovered that something was going wrong in the shop. The head of the whole Group's Security Branch came down and called all the black staff into the canteen in parties. He gave them all an ultimatum about stealing and said he was going to send his security men in at any time, unannounced, to search all the Africans.

Steven says, "I was lucky to be in the last party called in. After the Security Chief had spoken, he asked, 'Any questions?'" Steven got up. He expressed shock at the Company's losses but said that stealing must be dealt with not as a colour problem but a heart problem. He wanted to work that employees really cared for the firm and that the firm should care for the employees as people. The Security Chief burst out, "But I have tried to help Africans in so many ways, and they just don't care," and off he went.

Steven thought a lot about this. He felt something must be done, or else management would go on deepening the division between black and white. So he wrote to the Security Chief. He agreed that new security rules were necessary, but wondered if they by themselves could solve the problem. He then told how he had discovered that change could come in a man's character and how it had happened to him. He suggested that this could be the aim of all the Group's branches and that in this way they could make a real contribution to the country.

During the next three weeks the security men came and made their searches. The fourth week, no sign of them. Nor the fifth week nor any time since. Steven wondered what had happened.

One morning, as he asked God for guidance, he was convinced he ought to see this man again. He went straight to Head Office and found the man in. The Security Chief immediately said how much he had appreciated his letter and had read it several times. "Do you still see the security men in your shop?" he asked. It turned out it was the one shop from which they had been withdrawn.

Steven then said that he had not come to see him about that, but about the poor quality of food in the canteen which was arousing much feeling! Straight away the boss called his right hand man. He introduced Steven as "fighting for justice". Together they talked it over and an investigation was promised. Steven returned to the shop, went straight to his manager and told him what he had done. He was amazed at his manager's response. Soon the quality of food improved dramatically.

As I sat under a big tree outside the supermarket during the lunch break hearing Steven tell what had happened within a few months, the straight look in his eye told its own story. Here was a young man free of the confines of any system.

He and his friends, black and white, are taking what they are learning far and wide through their own country. They have been down to South Africa. He has met white Cabinet Ministers and black nationalist leaders. He is not going to sit back and let events decide his future. He is going to build it himself.

10. A SCHOOLMASTER'S HOME

3 000 kilometres south of Salisbury is Somerset West, a sleepy little town set between the Hottentots Holland mountains and the great sweep of False Bay, 50 kilometres from Cape Town. One could not visualise it as a natural storm centre of debate. Yet, in recent months, it has become just that. It is also the home of a family who are taking surprising initiative.

Like all old settlements in the Southern Cape the history of Somerset West goes back several centuries. From the beginning white and coloured – that is those of mixed race of whom there are over two million in South Africa – built the town together, mostly living in self-contained areas, though in some parts intermingled.

In the 1960's the Government went ahead with its policy of establishing clearly defined areas separating white and coloured. They declared that people would develop better apart and that occasions for friction would be removed. However, the Government-appointed Theron Commission, which has just tabled a massive Report on brown/white relations recommending far-reaching changes, says that the Group Areas Act embodying these ideas has increased bitterness, because the coloured people regard it as "inhuman".

Somerset West has now focussed this issue. Many old established coloured families there did not quite believe that the Government would implement the Act in all its detail to their town. Then, early in 1976, the blow fell. Notices to move were served. One family affected was that of Peter and Shirley Gordon.

The Gordons have been in the area since 1833. They were

among the first owners of land there. A half-page article in the Cape *Argus* describes them as "one of Somerset West's best-known coloured families".

Under the headline "A Moving Decision" the *Argus* reporter writes "Sitting in her attractive sitting-room with the sound of children's voices floating in from the swimming pool outside, Shirley Gordon spoke of the prospect of leaving her 18-year old home and the large property her family have owned for generations.

"Hers is only one variation of a similar story told by most of Somerset West's coloured residents, the story that motivated 3 000 whites in this conservative town to sign a petition demanding their coloured neighbours be allowed to stay."

I asked Peter Gordon if such spontaneous initiative had ever come from the whites before. "Not that I know of," he said. "Certainly to us in Somerset West it was totally unexpected. But this situation is being used to stir people's conscience."

Peter, Rev. Fourie, the Minister of his church, and others have taken much initiative themselves. "Four of us who lead the Action Committee on this issue approached the Government," he told me. "Rather to our surprise we found ourselves, a short time later, sitting down man to man with two Cabinet Ministers, the Mayor of Somerset West and the Dominee of the Dutch Reformed Church in the town. There was a spirit there that I had never expected. We are now hopeful of real change, though nothing has yet been officially announced. Much has still to be worked out and we pray that it will be."

A few days after this meeting *Die Burger*, the country's oldest Afrikaans newspaper, which supports the Government, wrote, "The growing apart of brown and white is something which causes many people disquiet. The worry about the removal of Somerset West's brown people spreads far and wide. The question arises whether the removal is really necessary".

The paper discussed the settled nature of the community with its 9 689 brown and 12 365 white. It continued, "Brown opinion is, today, much tougher than a decade ago. Brown men want all the more to have a say in deciding their own future. They believe that their claim to live in Somerset West is just as strong as that of the whites. They began the town together, they have always lived there. There is, for instance the Gordon family after whom Gordon Street, the Gordon High School and Gordon's Bay are named. They have helped their town develop. They pay their municipal taxes."

The *Argus* reporter was fascinated by another angle from the Gordons. She wrote, "If, after all, the Government stands firm by its mass-removal scheme Shirley and her husband Peter Gordon, who is Vice-Principal of a local primary school, have planned their course of action. "We're going to give our house away," Shirley said. "We don't want more fighting and bitterness about it than there already has been. We'd rather give our house to people who will love and appreciate it as much as we do."

"If the Gordons have to move," the *Argus* went on, "They are turning their house over to Moral Re-Armament."

Peter and Shirley are leaders in their Methodist Church. They say, "In the last year we have begun to think of ourselves not just in an isolated situation, but as one of a whole force of people from many backgrounds, important and unimportant, big people or small, going through the same kind of struggles in different circumstances."

It has been a new thing for them to meet in their home an Australian Presbyterian minister who has been both Secretary of the Australian Council of Churches and a Cabinet Minister in his country's Government; several white Dutch Reformed Church dominees; young men and women from Europe; black and white Rhodesians.

The Gordons have begun to look at things differently. Peter says, "I used to judge people in advance and put them in boxes. Now I can get things across to people because we started with change in ourselves". Shirley adds, "There are still attitudes and worries I don't know how to cope with but now I have hope for the future."

One thing which stirred them deeply had nothing to do with the colour problem. It concerned their daughter Gillian. Last December she finished her school career. She is a lively, intelligent girl, but her exam results were not good and her parents felt shut out from any real communication with her. Her father says, "She wanted to be a doctor in the black Homelands. But her maths results closed that door. Perhaps," he added, "it was a manoeuvre of God".

The family had got to know a Swedish girl and her parents who impressed them with their determination, together, to find God's will. Peter and Shirley wondered if what they talked about could help Gillian. They decided to raise her fare and send her to Europe in their care. It was a bold step. Neither they nor Gillian knew what to expect.

A month later Gillian wrote to them, and in the next weeks this letter became a talking point in Somerset West, for her parents showed it to everyone. The letter said:

"Dear Mum and Dad,

"I know I have caused you a tremendous amount of hurt and worry, especially this last year, and I am really sorry for it. I hope you will forgive me.

"This time here has made me think what I was really living for. And I found that my life has been completely empty. How selfish I had been wanting everything for myself and not caring what was happening in the world or even in the people around me . . .

"I've got to the point where I feel I should give my life to God, and do what He wants me to do, because He has a plan for everyone . . .to be able to feel other people's suffering and give all I can.

"I thought of my shyness and realised I was too afraid to say what I felt and give my own opinion because I was always worried about what other people would think of me. Therefore I have decided to become an individual under God and to serve and take my own initiative. Also daring to do things and be responsible . . .

"Thank you for all you have done for me . . .

Gillian".

When the notice of compulsory removal was served on the family and their thoughts turned to emigration, Gillian wrote again, "Do not be deserters and leave South Africa. You will be used for the benefit of others".

The Gordons say, "From the moment we decided to hand over the future of our home to God, all tension and bitterness left us".

Of course everyone hopes they can stay. Their neighbours in the same road, who are white, have told them they want them there. This has surprised Peter. "Sometimes when we argued over neighbourly issues like our dog I could have hit out and been rude," he said. "But I didn't. Now, you know, I am not afraid of apartheid any more, even if I think it is wrong."

The Gordons are already using their home in unexpected ways. Recently their big sitting room was filled with white students from Stellenbosch who came to meet Alec Smith and Rev. Kanodereka on their visit to the Cape. It was as new a thing for most of those whites to be guests in a coloured home as it was for the Gordons to have them.

This was soon followed by two further occasions. At the latest one, just after the serious riots, fifty people packed in. In the course of the evening a coloured student spoke. He told how, earlier in the week, he had been involved in what he considered a peaceful and unprovocative protest march, but had been beaten and battered by police batons. For three days he had been flamingly bitter and had taken it out on every white man he met. Several times he had almost telephoned to refuse the Gordons' invitation because he knew there would be whites there.

Then he had met an Afrikaner, a lecturer at the University, who had defended nothing, but had listened with tears in his eyes and taken on himself the wrongs committed. This brought the student up with a jolt. He had seen how reactionary it was just to judge in terms of colour. He said simply, "I have had to ask God to forgive me and to set me on the right road again". One sensed his new-found freedom.

There was silence after he had spoken. Then an Afrikaner from a farming area turned to the coloured people there and said how sorry he was for the inbred arrogance in men like him which caused such feeling.

A coloured minister said, "Up till tonight, when I asked myself, 'Who is my neighbour?' I always thought of my fellow brown man. From tonight I know the white man is my neighbour too". So it went on, as the deepest things in people came to the surface.

A few days later Peter had a letter from one of the Stellenbosch students, who described himself as that most solid of Afrikaners, "a born and bred Free Stater". "Thank you for helping me to clear out so many misunderstandings from my life. I feel so powerless, but these days I have learnt to live with new hope and fire. I am dead certain that you have done more in three evenings for this land and its people than I have done in a whole year's national service with the parachute battalion". He asked Peter to visit him at home.

Peter's minister, the Rev. Fourie, invited the Rev. Kanodereka to preach in their church in Somerset West during their visit. It was one of those evenings one will never forget. Members of black and white congregations joined the coloured people to jam the church to its doors. The singing had a full-throated quality that gripped. Kanodereka spoke first. Then he called on Alec Smith. And he unexpectedly asked a white Dutch Reformed Church dominee to come up from the body of the congregation to give the closing prayers.

Rev. Fourie said afterwards, "You have no idea what an evening like this has done for Somerset West". It had been a tough week for him as a coloured man, and for his people, he said. Official negotiations were proving sticky and spirits were low. Some of his people, too, had felt rejected by the whites when they went to the burial service of a white man many of them had known.

These things go deep. But so also did the choir when they sang that night,

"So send I you to bind the bruised and broken,
O'er wand'ring souls to work, to weep, to wake;
To bear the burdens of a world made weary,
So send I you to suffer for My sake.

"So send I you to leave your life's ambition
To die to dear desire, selfwill resign;
To labour long and love where men revile you,
So send I you to lose your life in Mine.

"So send I you to hearts made hard by hatred,
To eyes made blind, because they will not see;
To spend, tho' it be blood to spend and spare not,
So send I you to taste of Calvary."

11. THREE DOMINEES

Prime Minister Vorster and many others speak of the move towards change in South Africa. If this is to happen, the Dutch Reformed Church must play a key – perhaps *the* key – part. For the Church is the heart and soul of Afrikanerdom which holds all the reins of power and it feels itself the keeper of the country's conscience. So, rightly, the dominees of the Church carry great weight. And among them there is increasingly outspoken debate about fundamental issues.

I think, for instance, of a series of sermons given by Professor W. D. Jonker, Professor of Dogmatics and Ethics at the Dutch Reformed Theological Faculty at Stellenbosch University during Mission Week in 1975. This week is the high point in the Church Year in Stellenbosch, the cultural home of Afrikanerdom, where four of the last five Prime Ministers have graduated. Mr. Vorster is Chancellor of the University.

During Mission Week three thousand students and staff pack the historic Sentraalkerk and neighbouring halls for six successive evenings to hear a challenge from one of their spiritual leaders. For someone from the secular atmosphere of European university life it is an eyeopener.

The professor, of course, covered a wide field in six sermons. At one particular point he spoke of the need for his people to look at themselves through the eye of the black man. What must go through the heart of the black man when he sees what some church members do? What does he think of his treatment in shops and offices, or as he reads the newspapers?

The professor referred to the bitterness towards black members of the Dutch Reformed Church on black university campusses. They are turned out with the abuse, "You are the white man's dogs". "If we open our eyes and ears", the professor said, "we will hear these things. We don't need, in the first instance, to go and listen to the violent critics or to the out-and-out radicals. Let us just listen now and then to what our own people say, our own black members of our church.

"According to an opinion poll," he went on, "only one percent of the black people think of the Afrikaners as peace-loving people, while the overwhelming majority consider us impolite, cruel and heartless. We are often quick to say, 'What you think is not true. It is incitement that has made you think of us like that. It is our enemies that have whipped you up against us. There are all kinds of agitation that lie behind your feelings about us'.

"Certainly we have never intended many of the things which are ascribed to us. At the same time, even if we are convinced that there is a great deal of misunderstanding about this, *we must enquire into our way of doing things.*"

When one meets Professor Jonker, one realises that such words are not spoken easily. It takes immense courage, anywhere in the world, for a thinker to draw attention to unpalatable opinions. In his rather worn look one senses the struggle it is for this quiet, scholarly man to express what he feels God is telling him to say. As he put it in one of his sermons, "If I was disobedient this week and did not speak about these things, I would be doing no favour to you nor to our land".

He discussed the need to respect another man's values and identity without demanding "you must first become white, you must first become as I am, you must first accept *my* identity.

"It is for us", he said, "simply to cease thinking that I am better than the other man just because I am of another colour.

"It is a tremendous challenge placed before us as a Church of Christians to show that, perhaps for the first time in history, it truly can be done."

Professor Jonker also talked of fear. He asked, "Can the black man and the brown man always see in my life that I am set free by the message that I preach? Can he see in our lives the freedom of the children of God? Can he see in our lives that we are free from fear? Or can he rather see how concerned we are about ourselves, how fearful we are about what will happen to us, how worried about guarding our identity, how frightened what will result if we truly are full of friendship and love towards him?

"It is impossible that a man be gripped by the love of Christ and yet stay the same in his own life and in society. We have repeatedly said this week that the example of Our Lord Jesus Christ in so many instances in the Bible is held up before us not just as an example that we *must* follow, but as an example which, through the power of the Holy Spirit, we *can* follow."

The professor moved quickly from principle to practice. "I must not push in front of another man at the counter because he is not white. I must draw attention to it if a black man is waiting before me to be served. I must not humiliate another man. I must see to it that in no single instance are other people's feelings hurt."

Referring to the need for change in society to mirror change in individuals the professor told the story of a South African born lady who came back to visit her sister on the farm. She looked around her at the house, the equipment, the two cars in the garage. "You certainly are well-to-do here in South

Africa," she said. "What's wrong with that?" answered her sister. "We have the money and there are no poor people here."

"Yes, certainly there were no poor white men there," commented the professor. "But many poor people do live among us. They are of a different colour. But often *their* poverty does not affect us. We have become accustomed to it. But Christian love must make this seem strange. Christian love must make us open our eyes to our neighbours' interests."

The Afrikaner has long turned to his Church as his rock and his guardian against the threat of outside cultures. Professor Jonker ended by emphasising the Church's full, outward-looking mission.

"I want further to ask you to understand what lives in the heart of the Church," he said. "When it was the Afrikaner who was poor the Dutch Reformed Church picked him up. The Church has always understood its task as putting the preaching of the Gospel above everything. It is in accord with this spirit of the Church if we can understand that now is the time to grasp each other's hands and say, 'In the name of the Lord Jesus Christ we are going to take on ourselves the weakness of those who are not strong and not consider what pleases us'."

IN CAPE TOWN

Chris Greyling lives in Cape Town. His particular calling as a dominee brings him constantly into touch with brown as well as white. It gives him day to day contact with all that seethes in the people around him. He feels it deeply. I have seen him in near despair after reading the morning newspaper, the horror in the news and the prejudice, fear and bitterness in the letter columns. What can be done which goes deep enough and fast enough?

He is a man of learning. But perhaps his hope rests as much on his own experience of God at work as it does on his doctorate or his biblical studies.

A little while ago he and I spent the evening together with two senior coloured leaders. Talk turned, as always, to South Africa. At first Chris did not say much. Then something prompted him to tell us of landmarks in his own life.

He grew up on a farm in the Transvaal with a great love for his own people and a great deal of prejudice against the English and the urbanised blacks. The rural blacks he felt he could understand. They were his friends. "Basically that meant I only trusted black people who remained in an inferior position," he said. "The white man had to remain in his place and the black man in his. Once the black man started wearing a dark suit, carrying a briefcase and speaking English instead of his own vernacular – then he became a danger, an enemy."

While in his first year at University Chris had to face deep change in his life, and God – as if with His own sense of humour – used English, urbanised blacks and an Indian to open his eyes to wrong in his own life and the lives of his people.

One evening Chris was invited to the home of a dentist friend. Four young people from Scotland, England and the United States told stories of what had happened in their lives. Their conviction struck Chris. They clearly had something to live for – and he wanted it. But each time he spoke to them his English seemed to leave him in the lurch. He felt as if his tongue was tied in knots. Still, it was a decisive evening for him. A new honesty about himself and what needed to be different was born.

Shortly afterwards, Chris and some other students from Pretoria University were invited to join the cast of the play "The Forgotten Factor" (which had triggered the change in the life of Basil Kew, the farmer) when it went to Kenya and Uganda. There, several people had a profound effect on the young Afrikaner. One was an Indian businessman from the town of Eldoret.

Chris had grown up in an area where the Afrikaners were encouraged, in church and school, to boycott Indian shops. But in Kenya he was asked to go ahead of the main party to Eldoret to help prepare for the play coming – and the man he was to work with was Jethabhai Patel.

"In Jethabhai I met a man whose sole aim was to live in obedience to God," Chris said. "He suffered many insults from whites, but he remained free from bitterness and hate. He invited us for supper. It was my first meal in an Indian home. I was deeply impressed.

"That evening, when I had my time of quiet, I had to confess to God my racial pride and prejudice and to see it as a sin. If God could change a man to the stature of Jethabhai Patel, who was I to hate him or think myself superior just because I had a white skin? That was a landmark in my life."

In Nairobi Chris stayed with a medical doctor and his wife. She was seriously crippled, often in pain and confined to a wheelchair. In spite of this she was always caring for others, writing letters of encouragement and, with the telephone next to her bed, helping with the organisation of the play.

At one point Chris found himself separated from his fellow-Afrikaners and working with a hot-tempered and very English character. One day, at the booking office, everything got too much for Chris and he left, very disgusted, very lonely and very sorry for himself. He felt like going back to South Africa.

When he got home, tea was served in his hostess' room where she was sitting in considerable pain. Chris said, "I came into that room terribly conscious about myself and the way I was wronged. I asked Caroline how she was. She said simply, 'No, Chris, I was a little naughty this morning and the Lord has just spoken to me about it'.

"What do you mean?" he asked.

"This morning I was very sorry for myself. And the Lord showed me that if you are sorry for yourself, you cannot be sorry for anybody else," she said.

There Chris stood, a strong, healthy young man with his whole life and future ahead of him. There was Caroline, paralysed, bound to a wheelchair, barely able to move and, that day especially, suffering heavy pain. Yet she felt she had failed by being full of self-pity!

"I went to my room, but it was too small for me," Chris continued. "I went for a long walk into the forest nearby and there, with a long line of safari-ants in a row six inches wide and as far as the eye could see, I knelt down and was honest to God not only about the self-pity of that day, but for a whole life that had been full of self-pity because of growing up in a poor home with a drinking father.

"I thought of all the ways I had tried to compensate for my feeling of inferiority by putting on a mask of being a jolly fellow, while inside self-pity filled me. Since that time I have always seen it for what it is – a paralysing sin. In Caroline's words, 'If you are sorry for yourself, you cannot be sorry for anybody else'."

In Nairobi Chris and the others had heard a great deal about a man called Kenyatta. This was shortly before Mau Mau days and people talked of this man who was "persona non grata" to the British authorities who looked on him as a dangerous agitator. Perhaps this gave Chris and his fellow-Afrikaners a fellow feeling!

Chris and one of his friends called on an African whose name they had been given. As they talked they mentioned that they would be interested to meet Mr. Kenyatta. "That's lucky," their host said, "I am expecting him here any moment."

A few minutes later in he walked.

He was startled and somewhat suspicious to meet white South Africans in his friend's home. Chris and his colleagues told him what they were doing and what they were learning for themselves and for their country. Something must have caught his attention because, when the play opened a few days later in the Civic Theatre, the British Governor was in the the front row downstairs and Kenyatta in the front row of the balcony upstairs, with a cross-section of Kenya in between. The developments from there are a story in themselves.

Kenyatta went a step further. He invited the South Africans to visit one of his schools and to have lunch with him in his home. This was a further stretch for Chris to accept. Kenyatta took them around the classrooms. Later the whole school was brought out on parade and Kenyatta himself interpreted for Chris and his friends when they spoke to the children of what they were living for. Then Chris sat down to a meal with a man who was to be one of the future leaders of Africa, though at that time regarded as a danger by all in authority. "That is one chicken I shall never forget eating," Chris says.

When Chris and his colleagues returned to Pretoria not everyone understood what they were up to. Some said they had become "political". But Chris' concern was that men hand over total authority to God. It was up to Him what happened from there.

He kept looking for God's fresh initiatives. One morning he had the thought, "Go and meet Dr. Nkomo". Now it was one thing to see black nationalists in Kenya, but quite another to do so in Pretoria. Nkomo was known as one of the most militant men in South Africa. With others he had founded the African National Congress Youth League because he thought the parent body was going too "hat-in-hand" to the authorities.

Nkomo said, "The students came to my house. It was unusual, to say the least. It was not the "done" thing. They said they had been wrong to adopt an attitude of racial superiority towards us on the basis of colour, and that they wanted a basis of unity founded on listening to the voice of conscience and the idea not of who is right, but what is right.

"There seemed to be no point in preparing myself to shed the blood of such people," Nkomo said. "They seemed genuine. It would be reactionary to maintain the old stand."

The students invited Nkomo to the conference in Lusaka at which his life took a new turn. It was a move which was to affect not only his own people in South Africa but other African countries in the years to come.

Little did Chris realise where God was leading. It is this possibility of a chain reaction of change which gives hope and purpose today. Chris says, "I have been gripped by the way the prophets, when they were alone with God, would cry about the sins of their nations with a deep compassion, confessing not only personal but national sin. They had the courage to speak boldly without fear of man.

"The way of the Cross, for me, is not in self-righteousness

to blame others, but in humility to accept both our sin and the change which God can give, with prophetic boldness."

It is quite an experience to go into the South African Parliament or a government office with Dominee Daneel. Everybody seems to know him. Perhaps it is not only due to his standing as a minister of the Dutch Reformed Church. He also happens to have played rugby for South Africa and was recently chosen by an expert as one of a Springbok team of all-time greats.

Daneel not only seems to be known by everyone, but to be related to most of them. The Murray family, of which he is part, has enormous ramifications. This is not surprising when you learn that the original Rev. Murray who came out from Scotland to take a DRC post in South Africa had eleven children, of whom five boys became dominees and four daughters married dominees!

This is another way in which Afrikanerdom reminds me of Ireland. You only have to talk for a few minutes to find some family connection. It makes for a very closeknit community. It creates strength. It is also not easy to stick your neck out.

In Ds. Daneel you feel a deep, abiding love of his people and country and a complete identification with them. It is a quality which, in its almost mystical depth, sets the Afrikaner apart from the average English-speaking South African.

In 1953 Ds. Daneel travelled North to the same conference in Lusaka, Zambia, at which Dr. William Nkomo found a new outlook. Daneel heard Nkomo speak of the true feelings of the black man. As he listened a door to new understanding opened for him. He says, "I suddenly realised that it was the arrogance of white men like me which caused the bitterness in men like Nkomo. I had to apologise and ask God to forgive me".

He and Nkomo became friends and began to work together. Later a new realisation of the stature of Nkomo grew in Daneel. He felt it was important that the white leaders of his country should meet him and grasp what a man like Nkomo saw for the future of South Africa. He knew he should make it possible for this to happen.

But it did not seem to work out. It was not then the accepted thing for white leaders to consult with black. Daneel found that the way did not open easily, so he desisted. Then Nkomo died.

This hit Daneel hard. He says, "I had not done what God had told me because I was still bound by fear of what my own people would think. I decided that, from then on, I was going to be completely at God's disposal no matter what the circumstances, no matter what my friends or my people would think".

Daneel had made a practice of giving God the first, early-morning hour of each day to ask what He wanted done. It meant a daily decision to let Him break all built-in reservations and fears.

One morning in 1974 Daneel felt that God prompted him clearly, "An international conference for the Moral Re-Armament of Southern Africa, for all races, and for all parts of Africa to be held in Pretoria". It seemed impossible. But Daneel had learnt to be obedient and not to rely just on his own comprehension.

With his new freedom from fear, doors opened in a remarkable way. The Government agreed it could happen. Delegates crossed borders normally closed, coming from Nigeria, Kenya,

Mozambique and further afield. Three Homeland Chief Ministers and leading Afrikaners were among 400 of all races who stayed for a week in a hotel in the centre of Pretoria. Many new insights were gained and decisions reached, for the emphasis was not on theory or resolutions, but on the experience that attitudes could change and new aims be found.

Since then Daneel, in addition to working closely with his own people, has frequently been asked for help by black leaders, some of them strongly nationalist. It is not a usual role for a dominee. They do not turn to him for politics. They sense in him a man who will help clarify what is right because he is uncompromising with himself. They know that fear, bitterness or self-concern will not go unchallenged. They respect the vision of a new, God-architected society which he holds up.

Daneel was musing about this recently. A Chief Minister from one of the Homelands had just asked to see him. "Why he should have asked for me I honestly don't know," Daneel says. "But I do know that, for me, there is now only one thing that matters. That is what God wants, that He actually is in charge; in charge of my life, my future, my time, my country. This takes priority and comes before every other loyalty, whatever it may be."

Ds. Daneel's wife tells how this is a decision that goes much deeper than relationships between black and white. At one point in his career Ds. Daneel felt he was meant to work for a God-led quality of leadership not only for his own country, deeply as he cared about that, but also wherever needed around the world. It was a difficult decision as it meant leaving the security of a congregation, salary and home.

Mrs. Daneel says, "I knew what it would mean. There would be no fixed income, no security of home or comfort, and with it the responsibility of three small children. I could not imagine God asking a thing like that. My whole being objected and rebelled. Fear took over. Like Jonah of old I tried to run away from God's plan for me and my family. It went on for a year. Life became strain and battle.

"Then God spoke in no uncertain terms; 'You cannot accept Christ only as your Saviour; you must accept Him as your Master too'. After a short time of quiet listening, it stood there before me in black and white, 'I have made a bogey of this decision, but now I see it was the devil's way of keeping me from giving my all to remake the world'.

"What a terrible thing it was to have been bound and gagged by fear for more than a year. Then what a miracle! The moment the deepest thing in my heart was brought out into the light, the evil control was broken and I was a free human being under God's control once more. This was the point – to hand over control. It felt like losing my whole life. And it went deeper because it involved my husband and children as well. A complete handover. For me it was 'whosoever will lose his life for My sake, the same will save it'."

At every opportunity Ds. Daneel puts his convictions to his own people. He spoke to the General Synod of the Dutch Reformed Church. The Editor of a British publication which reported his talk wrote in introduction, "This is not a political statement. It is moral and spiritual truth. Acceptance by us in Britain of its challenges would alter social, economic and political attitudes in *this* country. We, too, could then surprise the world".

Ds. Daneel said, "In its Report to the Synod, the Commission for Racial and Ecumenical Affairs states, 'In calling people to repentance and sanctification, the Church wants to create a new philosophy of life and a new world outlook which will be a strong tie between people across national barriers'.

"This is the time when such a call should go forth from the Church. The future of our country is in the balance. Changes are inevitable. The question is, what kind of change is it going to be: a voluntary change as the result of repentance or a violent change by force?

"Fear, however, should never be the main motive to put right what is wrong. We must do it because God wants it and because we are followers of Christ. To be reborn and obey the first command of loving God is no guarantee that we will love our neighbour, especially if he is black.

"Take the case of the Apostle Peter. He had advanced a long way in his Christian experience, a man filled with the Holy Spirit, yet he was in the grip of prejudice and superiority in his attitude to people of other races. He was still bound by tradition. In that state God could not use him to bring Christ's message to the Roman captain, Cornelius. A radical change had to take place in his attitude. That change did take place as the result of a vision God gave him, and he went into Cornelius' home having learnt that God is 'no respecter of persons'.

"Many of us feel we are free from race prejudice. But what about our fellow citizens of whom we often read in the newspapers that they ill-treat the blacks. They are our flesh and blood. As Christians we are called to identify ourselves with them as if we were equally guilty ourselves and need God's forgiveness.

"Of course Africans need to change as much as we do. But scripture teaches us first to remove the plank from our own eyes, then we will see properly how to take the splinter from our brother's eyes. We cannot allow our Afrikaner pride to prevent us from searching our own hearts and asking God to bring about the transformation in human relationships which our country needs.

"If we obey God, as St. Peter did, even when it clashes with our traditional way of life, we can trust Him with our own future and the future of all racial groups in this country."

Not long ago Daneel and a colleague visited a black leader, a vigorous nationalist, at the latter's request. He was a man at the centre of critical decisions and colossal pressures. Daneel and his friend had no sooner arrived than their host was interrupted by urgent visitors. "Oh my goodness," Daneel thought, "We are going to have no chance to talk."

But their host soon came back, took the two 'phones off their hooks, and then spoke completely frankly about things which he had told no-one else. He asked them to have a time when they sat quietly and asked God for His direction, because, as he said, "I have come to the end of knowing what to do".

"It is so easy," Daneel says, "to discuss, to argue, to calculate. It is something quite new as a basis of unity when political leaders can say, 'None of us know fully what to do. Let us, in a time of quiet, ask God to tell us what is right'.

"Of course it is a risk," Daneel says. "But is it more of a risk than the crises and deadlocks in which we find ourselves today? All I can say is that, that particular day, decisions were made with far-reaching consequences for the country. And that other decisions, made in the same spirit, have saved many lives."

12. A CHALLENGE IN THE COUNCILS

Pat Sonn moves in some of the high councils of South Africa. He is Chief Whip of the independent members of the Coloured Representative Council; he was one of the first three coloured men appointed to the Council of the University of the Western Cape and is now on the Executive Council; for his last nine years as a school principal he was Chairman of the Educational Council appointed by the State President to advise the appropriate Cabinet Minister; he was the one coloured assessor coopted on to the Cillie Commission of Enquiry into the recent wave of unrest in cities in the Transvaal and the Cape; and so on. The list does not end there.

Some critics might say, "He must be a government stooge". By no means. No one who knows him could say that. Why, then, does he accept the appointments? In answer, one must look at the complete picture of the man.

He is in his sixties now, balding, and he peers at you a little shortsightedly through his spectacles. He has always lived in an atmosphere of community leadership. His father, a carpenter, was a prominent figure among his people in the Karoo town of Carnarvon. Sonn, himself, when he qualified as a teacher, stepped straight into the principalship of a small school. From there he moved on to bigger schools, finally becoming headmaster of the Louis Rex Primary School in Queenstown. It was there that he faced his first major crisis.

He owned his own home in Grey Street, Queenstown, and was a pillar of the community, taking a leading role in educational, church and social life. The Group Areas Act was applied and he had to sell. He could not face the new set up in a town where he had been so settled and, in frustration, moved the 600 miles from the Eastern Cape to Cape Town where, in 1954, he bought another home, this time in Rondebosch, then an "open" suburb.

In 1960 the Group Areas Act caught up with him once more, and again he was told he must move. He and his wife have five children, four sons and an only girl. The daughter, rebelling against such insecurity, emigrated to Canada where she and her family now live. This went very deep with her father. He felt he could take no more. He wanted to hit out in hate at everyone and everything.

At that point he made a fundamental decision. "I had to choose," he says, "between being taken over by my bitterness and my reactions towards those who perpetrated injustice, or remaining free in my spirit to fight *for* change in those people who needed it rather than *against* them." This philosophy has become the cornerstone of Sonn's life. He does not minimise difficulties, but he has chosen deliberately to go to the heart of some of the toughest situations so as to work towards the change which he is convinced must come. He will use every platform to highlight what he feels are the basic moral issues, regardless of who is involved. Practically daily he has to go back to the sources of his faith for renewed strength, but, though often depressed and disheartened, he will not withdraw into the comfort of nursing bitterness.

One son, who himself is now President of the 7 000 strong Cape Teachers Professional Association, emphasises that this is not just a political tactic. Care for people and a concern for righteousness form the cornerstone of his father's life. It marks his dealings within his own family. When this son, in his younger days, borrowed the family car and did not return till late at night, leaving his parents stranded, his father looked at him straight and asked, "Was it right to do that?" "I felt so uncomfortable", his son says, "that I have always remembered that lesson. He made us feel he was dealing with the issue, not the person".

This approach has made him something of a catalyst during recent sessions of the Coloured Representative Council. A knowledgeable observer says that where, time and again, important issues would previously get sidetracked into personal slanging matches, Sonn, with his quiet, measured intervention, would bring members back to the point so that progress could be made. As one reads the record of the debates in the Council one is also struck with the impact of Sonn's humour, and how the word "Laughter" is often bracketed after his comments.

When Sonn feels that action is needed he does not hesitate to lift the 'phone and dial straight through to a Cabinet Minister or senior civil servant and, because they respect his integrity and his openness of spirit towards them, they listen. Sometimes they act, sometimes they don't. When they don't, Sonn has often to say to himself, "I will stick to my guns and go on fighting, and I will not be taken over by reaction".

Sonn finds increasingly that he has to put his personal position at risk in order to be uncompromising for what he feels is right. The University of the Western Cape is, perhaps, *the* focus of his people's struggle. Most of his community reject the concept of a separate institution of higher learning reserved for them. They want open opportunity. But, as it now exists, they have decided to use it as a stepping stone. They say, however, "If it is to be ours, then we expect the right to decide for ourselves how it should be run". They feel that, while the University Principal is now an able coloured academic, and many of the white staff are prepared to serve loyally, others still want to retain their own control.

This has centred on one recent issue. There has been a distinguished coloured professor on the university staff. By all accounts he is not an easy man to deal with in his personal relationships and he has been impatient in his demand for change. He has often clashed with some of his white colleagues and, indeed, has had reservations about Sonn and his methods of approach. Events came to a head late in 1976 when the professor's appointment was terminated by a Council decision in which all the coloured members (a minority) favoured confirming the appointment while all the whites, (with the notable exception of the Chairman) were against. It is not necessary here to try to judge the rights or wrongs of the case – and these facts come from a source other than Sonn himself – but what seems significant is Sonn's own action. Because he felt this a moral issue which needed to be fought, he put his personal position on the line. Though it was not the "done" thing, he considered they had been left no alternative but to take this to the country through a press statement. However, as some of his colleagues hold senior posts under the Government, he said to them, "I will take full personal responsibility for this", so that he would be the one to face any knocks that came.

The press statement takes issue with the structure of control in the firmest and clearest of terms. It represents the action of a man who is free from fear and free from self-interest; a man who does not pander to anyone, be they colleague or opponent.

Pat Sonn's eldest son, Franklin, is a national figure in his own right. He leads perhaps the most powerful single pressure group, the teachers. He is also constantly invited to diplomatic functions because his hosts know that he is quite uninhibited in expressing what his people feel.

Franklin is, by nature, a rebel. He questions everything. Like most of his generation he is outspoken in his demand for change. Till recently one subject, above all, dominated his thinking – how to shift his people's relationship with the white man in South Africa? But Franklin is also a thinker. He is prepared to put aside his reactions and look further than today or tomorrow. This was shown in a lengthy letter which appeared on 12th February 1977 in *Die Burger*, the paper read by the Afrikaner in the Cape. His letter is a forthright challenge to all colours. Some of the points he makes are:

"Tension in South African politics has taughtened phenomenally during 1976. Slogans and theories which, only yesterday, held great certainty now waver shakily in light of new realities. Never before has it been so important for South Africans of all races and convictions to put priorities first."

Sonn then lists some of these 'new realities' as he sees them. They include the seeming breakdown of the Rhodesian settlement plan, Russian involvement in Angola and President Podgorny's forthcoming visit to Zambia, Tanzania and Mozambique, international backing for anti-South African boycotts and for violence in South-West Africa, the run-down of South Africa's outward looking 'Africa policy', the United States' 'splendid isolation' and Prime Minister Vorster's New Year declaration that South Africa cannot rely on Western backing, so seatbelts must be tightened.

"Whether South Africa wants to recognise it or not," Sonn adds, "the 'Free West' sees in her, justly or unjustly, a threat to freedom itself."

"What does this situation hold for those of us who are not white?" asks Sonn. "Before black men rejoice in the fact that white South Africa is apparently at last being driven into a corner, they must take a good look at those through whom it has happened and in this perspective face their dilemma. On one hand we see and feel the weight of white domination with its impression that the maintenance of white power and white identity overshadows all other considerations. On the other we are forced to realise that it is Communist support for black movements which enables them to challenge white power in an armed struggle.

"But the black man who believes that he can tackle either the white man now or Communist domination later in a violent confrontation, relying on high-sounding moral slogans but without external military support, is as naive as the white man who believes he could emerge as overall victor of full-scale race war in Africa."

Sonn says that there is no dilemma for the black man who is ready to play along with Communism whatever the future cost in terms of Communist dictatorship or for the white man who withdraws to his 'laager' and sits there polishing his rifle, ready to fight to the end and die as a hero. Each has made his choice. But for the 'great, uncommitted, middle group *of all colours*' the dilemma is very real. Whatever our race or political viewpoint, our concern with our comforts or our fears, the eventual choice is going to be between the opportunism of Communism and a new concept of freedom. For this "middle group" the question of race identity becomes increasingly irrelevant.

"This is not to say," Sonn adds, "that the freeing experience of, for instance, 'black consciousness' is not important." But it, like 'white identity', will become less and less relevant in terms

110

of the longterm ideological struggle which will increasingly crystallise.

"This struggle," he says, "is our common responsibility, regardless of race. It means taking seriously the ideal of freedom and civilisation for all. For the white man it will mean abandoning oppressive measures and sacrificing his privileges and his fears on the altar of freedom. For the black man it will mean sacrificing his hurts, his recriminations, his exclusive black power."

Sonn asks for a united front of people, regardless of colour, who share the same conviction – that freedom and justice are as impossible under a Communist dictator as under a white one. "We must build together a new South Africa which transcends present divisions and boundaries. It will demand sacrifices from all sides."

13. THE COMRADE FROM COVENTRY

Early in 1942 a troopship on its way to Singapore stopped off in Cape Town. Among those who took the chance of a brief look at South Africa was a private in the Army Service Corps, Les Dennison. As he walked the Cape Town streets every bone in Dennison's body reacted to what he regarded as a classic case of "imperialist exploitation". For he was a committed Communist, totally dedicated to class war and world revolution.

In 1974 and '75 Dennison was back in South Africa, this time with a different angle, but with the same passion for change. It is instructive to look at his background and experience to get an understanding of the realities facing Southern Africa, for his 22 years in the Communist Party gives him a knowledge of what makes Communism work and what it will take to find an effective alternative. As far back as 1948 Dennison was given intensified training by the Party in the revolutionary potential of the African continent, so it is no new thing for him to think for this part of the world.

In 1974 he told a group of trade unionists and businessmen in Pretoria, "You have heard that word 'ideology'. Many of you don't like it, but you must understand it or you are irrelevant. I meet many people who talk of the danger of Communists; you sense the anti-Communist thing in them. They do not realise that Communism feeds on that kind of negative anti-Communism to gain the support of those it wants to win. If you are really concerned with answering Communism you have to blaze with a passion and a vision for the world so that the other man says, 'That is what I want'. It means going all out to work for the kind of continent you want to build, not just today, but next year and ten years ahead. How many of you think in those terms? It means living to win those opposed to you. Some men did that for me. That is why I am here."

When Dennison landed in Cape Town in 1942, his personal history made him super-sensitive to what he felt were wrongs in society. The hardships of his own upbringing had been appalling. In his home six children shared one bed, and he was surrounded by violence and degradation. As soon as he could, he got away from the house and went to work. At the age of 14 he was up at 3.00 a.m. to walk several miles to his shift in the mines. He earned R1 a week.

The 1926 General Strike was an early memory. He picked over the mine dumps for scraps of coal and queued for soup handouts. A consciousness of the exploitation of his class stirred within him and when he met Communism he responded to its call to smash the system. He took naturally to the discipline of the Party and soon found himself engaged in pitched battles with the fascists. He knew what it was to be beaten up while the police passively looked on.

By the time the war took him to Malaya he was a high-grade revolutionary. He had only joined the army when ordered to do so by the Party following Hitler's invasion of Russia. No sooner had he reached Singapore than the Japanese swept into that fortress. Dennison and thousands of others were captured amid accusations of inefficiency, self-seeking and even treachery which left him and his mates bitterly resentful.

The next three years were a mind-bending experience. He was drafted for work on the Burma/Siam "death" Railway. Most of his friends died in an agony of dysentery, or torture. But, amid the brutalisation, Dennison's discipline asserted itself and he kept up his Communist training. Though small, he is toughly built, but when he was finally released he weighed 5 stone 4 lbs, less than half his normal weight.

Back in Britain he became secretary of a party cell and one of the Communist elite. Despite a wife and children, he would be ready for action by 6.00 a.m. each morning, distributing 150 copies of the "Daily Worker" before starting work. Wherever he went he promoted industrial chaos. The Party directed him to the Standard Motor Company and, in 1956, he and his cell brought 13 000 men out on strike for three weeks. He was sacked, blacklisted by many employers, and on the dole for seven months. Finally he got a job as a plumber with the Coventry Corporation's housing programme.

One day, out on the site, a plasterer called Stan, who was working with him burst out in fury to Dennison, "You talk about revolution, but you are the biggest, bloody reactionary I've ever known. The workers don't like you. And what about the people who need these houses? You're sabotaging them. And how do you hope to unite the labour movement when you've got a divided home?"

This made Dennison blazingly angry, but it got under his skin because he recognised its truth. When Stan, who was a committed Christian, invited him to meet some of his friends he went along. These men put their faith to Dennison in terms of a revolution that went further than Marxism and which included all classes. They said that if individuals change, then society can change. This was a new concept to Dennison who believed that everything was determined by a man's environment. But it was not so much the intellectual reasoning that intrigued Dennison as the genuine care he felt in these men, combined with their discipline and all-out commitment.

No one told him what to do, but they challenged him that any truly just society must be based on certain absolute standards of morality. Dennison saw the point, but rejected any idea of God. They did not argue, but suggested he try listening honestly to what his conscience said.

He agreed to try, but when the first idea which occurred to him was to put things right with his eldest son Karl (named after Marx), whom he had thrown out of the house, he resisted. Finally he summoned up his courage and took the first step. To his astonishment it worked. Slowly his family was reunited and a faith began to be born. He says, "I had spewed out doctrinaire ideas of world brotherhood, but here was practical evidence of the irreconcilable being reconciled".

He did not become soft or sentimental. His outspoken fight for change continued. Meanwhile the Russian invasion of Hungary and the exposures about Stalin had shaken him. His fresh personal discoveries made him further question the dictates of the Party, so he resigned. Soon afterwards some of his new friends invited him to travel with them to meet workers and industrialists in India. As Dennison was brought face to face again with grinding poverty, his passion to bring an adequate change to injustice and exploitation everywhere deepened. But India also brought back to him all the brutalities of the years in Malaya, some of which he himself had perpetrated. He felt it was too much to bear and sank into depths of despair. He talked of this with a friend, a shipyard worker. The next morning his friend said, "What you need is forgiveness" and suggested he read Psalm 51 in the Bible. Dennison says that, that day, he felt Christ's second touch and a fresh faith began to grow. Now that faith is the firm foundation of Dennison's life.

When he came to Pretoria in 1974 to take part in the conference called by Ds. Daneel, he was passionately concerned that white and black go deep enough and far enough in what they should live for to enable them to build a society able to challenge the indulgent materialism of the West and the dedicated materialism of the East. He talked of what was needed to train men and women to go beyond goodwill and good works so that they dealt with the most fundamental issues. He spoke one morning to a number of employers of his experiences in industry. He talked of the time the Party had directed him to the job in the Standard Motor Company. "We used to have marvellous strikes there," he said. "If we did not have an issue I would say to my comrades, as secretary of the party cell, 'Leave it for a couple of days. Those fools of bosses, they'll make a wrong move'. And you could rely on it that, within two days, if you wanted an issue, they would give it to you. We could count on their blindness and their arrogance.

"I say to bosses, 'How do you build trust with those on the other side of the fence'? I say to Government, 'How do you build trust with those opposed to you'? I don't just think of the political level. How do you build trust, man to man? Those bosses in the Standard Motor Company never understood that the issues which were laid on the table were never the real point. Reality was what churned me and my comrades up inside. If those bosses were to be ahead of the game, they needed to learn what made us tick, why we felt as we did, and how to deal with that.

"Effective leadership means learning to do this. In any negotiating situation you have to reckon with the problems sitting *around* the table if you are going to answer the problems

116

on the table. Communism's strength is that it knows how to exploit the bitterness, fear and greed in men, while the non-Communist acts as though these were not there, did not matter, or will, if ignored, go away. It was a wise man who said, 'Cabinets, to rule well, must learn the art of changing men'."

14. GOING OR STAYING?

Many Afrikaners deeply distrust the English-speaker. They regard his roots in Africa as shallow. They believe he is liable to up sticks and go when trouble looms.

After recent riots one could hear a number of comfortably-off Capetonians discussing the relative merits of Australia or Canada, New Zealand or Ireland as escape routes. But that is just a small part of the story. When you meet the descendants of the 1820 British settlers to South Africa you realise how they pride themselves on their South Africanism and what a contribution to the country they have made. The opinion columns of the Afrikaans press also make it clear that talk of emigration is not confined to the English.

Yet there is a seed of truth in the accusation. It is often said that the wealthy, mainly English-speaking, city suburbs can afford their "liberal" image because they could buy themselves out of trouble. Certainly some of the liberalism perished in the riots. Polarisation was immediate when comfort was threatened.

This vicious circle of action and re-action can, however, be broken — and by typical city business types as much as anyone.

Don Barnett is a hard-driving chartered accountant in industry. He is only 27, but when you see his lovely house in the Salisbury suburbs, with its sweep of green lawn and brimming flowerbeds, you get the impression of someone who has "arrived".

Early in 1976 Don was driving home with his wife Penny and their two rumbustious young sons from a family holiday in Natal. Instead of feeling refreshed, he was depressed. He says, "I had been on security force duty in the operational area and seen the growing rift between the races. Those we are fighting often wear no uniform. Others assist them, some voluntarily, some under threat of death. In these circumstances the whites, understandably, become suspicious of every black man. The blacks, of course, sense this and react".

It was the time of the Smith/Nkomo talks. As they drove home, Don said to Penny, "Look, I just don't see an end to this. If these talks don't produce something I think we should consider moving down to Natal". Penny felt much the same.

"My sons are third generation Rhodesians," Don said. "I always hated to think I might be prepared to ditch my country which we love very much. Yet we had got to this point. Then the talks failed."

Don stopped for a moment and looked at Penny. We were in their sittingroom with the scarlet and white bougainvillea cascading over the patio outside. It was very still in the heat of the day.

"It was about this time that something happened which resulted in our staying here," Don went on. "In these last months there has grown in me a sense of responsibility that I need to earn a better society, a better life for our children and for this country. A friend told us the other day of someone they met recently in England, who said, 'Rhodesia is a great place. If things sort themselves out there, we will be the first to go back'. I know that some who have left the country have had good reasons, which I can appreciate. Others merely move from pasture to pasture, expecting to reap but never prepared to sow. It was Penny who started us in a new direction."

Penny: "I began to realise how dissatisfied I was with a life which seemed an endless stream of tea parties. I had heard some friends talk of God giving a new direction. One day I told Don of the searching in my own heart and my decision to try this. He was vaguely interested, but left it at that.

"I felt that my whole aim in life changed. I wanted so badly for him to share this, but I knew that to try and talk him into it would only put him off. I read one day in the Bible, 'Wives, if you believe and your husband does not believe, you will not win him by words, but by your actions'. I realised how much I nagged Don. I stopped this. It seemed to have an effect."

Don: "I went with Penny to meet some friends of hers who had started her new thinking. Two of them especially interested me – Bremer and Agnes Hofmeyr. He had been a Rhodes Scholar. Agnes was one of the Leakey family from Kenya. Her father had been murdered by Mau Mau because they needed the best man they knew for a sacrifice. I thought I would lose all faith in humanity if that happened to me. But she had decided she must not be made useless through bitterness, but must forgive and go on to build something better.

"A week or so later we were invited to dinner by these friends. I was still wary. I came late from work and when I arrived the guests were already at the table. Suddenly I realised that a black couple was among them. It was the first time I had ever sat down to a meal with a black person! Looking back now it seems so ridiculous, but I can remember that dinner vividly. Although I had always thought I was completely open-minded towards the blacks, I realised what little meaningful contact we had ever had and just how fundamental the lack of understanding was. Over coffee I asked the African guest about some questions on the minds of many whites. My friends kid me now that I was arrogant. I did not mean to be.

"I met another guest that evening who had had thirty years experience in the British Colonial Service and then in independent Africa. I told him my feeling about black Africa. My grandparents were refused a pension in Zambia and had had to leave after a lifetime's work. I had also lived in Malawi and saw things I did not like there. I felt deeply about these things. My fellow guest then said something which took me right off guard. 'Isn't it just possible that Rhodesia could work out something new, something better, which you could show to the rest of Africa and the world'?

"Perhaps it was my pride, but I responded to that. It seemed to turn a key in my mind. I began to look at some basic questions. What was my aim in life? What really mattered? I wanted happiness in my work and family life – how was I going about this?

"You see, although I had never known poverty, my family was not well off and I guess I yearned for the material things that many of my friends enjoyed. When I wanted to go to university I could not afford it. I could barely keep myself when doing my accountancy training so I decided that, come what may, I was going to be comfortably off and my goal became the next salary increment. 'When I qualify', I thought, at first, 'I'll earn a decent salary and then will begin to live'. We would have a better car, a house, that would earn the admiration of our friends, etc . . ."

Don shrugged his shoulders. "I qualified, my salary went up progressively, but I found I was still moody and self-centred. I snapped unnecessarily at Penny and the children, while at work innumerable things irritated me. Worst of all I knew what I was doing but felt powerless to alter it. So there we were – in search of happiness which always seemed just out of reach.

"After that dinner I started to think afresh. I saw the logic of a society based on absolute standards of honesty, purity, unselfishness and love – given that human nature can be changed. Things began to shift in me. I am a long way from sainthood, but my motives today are a far cry from six months ago. I began a scientific adventure of experiment and proof."

Penny: "My parents now say, 'The one thing we cannot get away from is the change in Don'. To me it was, perhaps, these personal, family things which meant most."

Don: "I was caught by this idea of building a new sort of country. Our usual way of doing things reminds me of the man who went to a gallery to buy a painting. He told the salesman that he knew what he liked and needed no assistance. The salesman asked, 'Do you know what you like or just like what you know'?

"This applies to so many of us. We are afraid to go beyond what we know. Our dinner parties, for instance, were always for the same round of friends. To move beyond this meant dealing with our basic fears. When the suggestion first came up of having a black man to our home I said, 'No way! What would our neighbours think? What about my business colleagues'?

"The funny thing is that once we made the start, others began to regard it as normal. One white friend, whose life is a round of wining and dining, said as he left one party, where he had met black and white, 'The most interesting evening for years!'

"I met this ex-Communist, Les Dennison. He told us of the Communists planning years ago for the takeover of Africa. Now it is one thing to throw up your hands in horror and say, 'How awful!' But do we in the West, we Christians, have an ideology to match this? Do we have a superior philosophy which we are prepared to live with as much conviction? Do we have a more effective plan to build together towards the 'New Society'?

"Against this background Penny and I went with fourteen other Rhodesians, including white businessmen, black nationalists and teachers to the Caux conference in Switzerland. There we joined people from all over the world.

"I was fascinated to meet Dr. Frederik Philips, President of Philips Electrical Industries and similar employers from Britain, Germany, Italy, Norway and other countries. These men believed that industry could and should meet the needs of society. I had been debating in my mind how industry could develop a 'social conscience'. We discussed problems like inflation, labour relations, the energy crisis. These men, with others from the trade unions, related examples of how new approaches were being made to some very old problems. I saw clearly how seemingly complex problems are all too often the results of – or aggravated by – personal greed, dishonesty and ambition. These men, who spoke from personal experience showed how, through dealing with basic human nature practical answers could be worked out."

Penny: "Meanwhile I met some of the wives. One morning I told of an instance of what absolute honesty meant in the family. I had been earning cash from giving private lessons at home. I kept the proceeds for my private extravagances. I think I have seventeen crochet books on my shelves!

"Then I thought that if I was going to be honest, it had to be in every situation and that we needed to pay the tax due on these earnings. I suggested this to Don. He said, 'Heavens! They will only laugh at you if you bring up this sort of thing.

123

Everyone does it.' But some months later Don did decide we should pay it.

"I told the ladies this story. A few days afterwards I was chatting with a black Nigerian lady. She introduced me to her husband who turned out to be the head of one of the Employers Organisations in Nigeria. 'Oh!' he said, 'You are the young lady my wife told me about. What you said about your husband and the taxes really went to my heart. When I get home I think there are some taxes *I* must pay'.

"That really struck me; that the conscience of a black Nigerian could be roused by the story of a white Rhodesian!"

Don: " This all links together. Take the issue of corruption – in Africa it is accepted as inevitable. The World Bank and other such bodies are concerned about its crippling effect on aid programmes and Third World Development. Western industrialised society certainly does not set a glowing example, but I believe that we in industry and commerce can and must provide an answer to corruption and division.

"The overall task is enormous, yet ordinary men and women have a part to play. It takes a personal commitment to national responsibility; to be part of the answer rather than part of the problem.

"It is not all plain sailing. The temptation 'Not to become involved' is always there. But we have made our decision – whereas last year we were ready to leave, now we are staying."

15. A SAXOPHONIST STEPS OUT

If you were to think of a South African who might influence men in Oxford University on one hand and Black Power on the other, you would be unlikely at first glance to choose Sam Pono. Short in stature and quiet in manner, he would pass unnoticed in a crowd.

Sam grew up in Queenstown on the border of the Ciskei in the Eastern Cape. Though he was an answer to prayer, he did not act like one. Sam's mother remained childless for so long after her marriage that she said to God, "If you give me a child I will dedicate him to You". In due course Sam was born, but he soon rebelled against his mother's expectations. He got in with a wild crowd and, even as a youngster, street fights and knifings were part of his life.

When he was twelve his parents decided to remove him from the town influences. They sent him to stay with a strict aunt at a rural mission station. He went to school there.

At seventeen he returned to Queenstown to take his Junior Certificate. Immediately all the old influences reasserted themselves. His behaviour stopped him pursuing further studies at college.

Sam's family was musically gifted. His uncles all played instruments. He learnt the saxophone, made good progress and soon was part of the most popular band in town the "Modern Jazz Sextet". They were in great demand in the night clubs, black and white, and Sam was swept, very willingly, into that life. Drink flowed, often to the detriment of musicianship, and girls fell into his lap.

He had a good job by day and the band by night, so he made

money. But life was expensive. Some shebeens allowed him credit and, by the week's end, his drink bill would be more than his salary. And the girls were not cheap.

When not out on the tiles, Sam lived at home. So that he would not have to contribute so much to the family budget he told his parents he was only earning half the true sum. Still his debts mounted. His father wanted to throw him out of the home, but his mother insisted that he stay.

Sam felt he deserved only the best. He bought a beautiful saxophone from a family friend. This friend would not trust Sam's credit. So without telling his father, Sam bought it in his name. One night at a drunken party someone fell on the saxophone and smashed it. Sam then refused to go on paying the instalments he still owed. This case, like others, ended up in court.

Meanwhile Sam was growing more and more politically conscious and anti-white. In the clubs he saw the whites at play. They were his bosses, but their messy living shocked him. It never crossed his mind that his own was similar.

A white band also played on the club circuit. Sam regarded them as musically inferior, but their earnings for similar engagements were far higher. This stoked his bitterness.

Meanwhile a powerful Queenstown character, Miss Eginah Mzazi, had made Sam an object of particular attention. She was a social worker and she confronted him with the damage he was doing to his family and people. Sam reacted to what he saw as a "holier than thou" approach, and continued on his way.

Miss Mzazi was also politically active. She had been a close colleague of Dr. Nkomo in the African National Congress. When Nkomo spoke of the need to cure bitterness as well as exploitation, she attacked him. But she watched him closely and became convinced that he was right.

She looked afresh at her own life and then came back to Sam with a different approach. "She was so humble. She even apologised to me for her previous attitude," Sam said. "She told me, 'Sam, I feel certain qualities in you which can contribute to the nation if they are harnessed rightly. But if wrong forces grip you, or you continue to destroy yourself with liquor and women, all that will be lost'."

Sam realised there was something new in Miss Mzazi. He was also interested in what she told him of a force of men and women around the world, determined to put right what is wrong, but with the courage to start with themselves.

Sam responded to this. His Christian upbringing began to become real for the first time. It involved changes. His first decision was to be honest with his father about his salary. His father was shaken. He said, "Sam, you've put me in a difficult position because I must be honest too. I have not been bringing all my salary home either".

They put all their cards on the table. His father had found it very hard to meet the cost of the younger children's schooling, rent, electricity and food. Sometimes their light was cut off.

"I had seen how much this hurt my parents," Sam said, "but I had never bothered". He apologised to his father for his selfishness and for abusing him when drunk. "It built a new family, because my brother and sisters had been copying me. Now they, too, began to change," Sam said.

Sam and his father pooled all they had. They paid off their debts. They started a joint savings account, and drew up a budget together. There were no more light cuts, and the children were no longer sent away from school because of unpaid fees. Even in the band a new discipline improved their music.

In 1973 Miss Mzazi and other friends suggested to Sam that he spent some time overseas to see how others were tackling the problems of their countries. They would help him pay his fare. His musician friends and others, black and white, joined in on this too.

As he travelled, Sam felt God gave him a clear commission. First was to care for those from all over Africa – Southern Africa, Uganda and so on – who live in exile. Secondly was to care for the descendents of the slaves who were taken from Africa.

"I was very scared," Sam says. "It seemed such an impossible task and I had no idea how to go about it. But I was led forward in an extraordinary way."

He found himself spending a year with an English family in Oxford. "I had never had a degree and felt very out of place. My only qualification was that God had given me this commission." In Oxford he got to know many people from all over Africa, Rhodes Scholars from South Africa and Rhodesia, the best students from Ghana and many others. "I felt if some of them could lay down their lives selflessly to see that their continent was truly cared for, that would do something for Africa."

He began to make friends with Afrikaner Rhodes Scholars and black exiles. "What helped me was to be honest with them. My experience of my own change was my greatest asset. One white South African said to me, 'You know, Sam, it's funny, but I trust you like my own brother'. Because I was ready to be honest with him, even about things of which I was very ashamed, he talked to me of the most real things in his life."

When he left Oxford four South African Rhodes Scholars gave him a big send-off party. Afrikaners, English, and black from South Africa spoke of what he had done for them and they gave him £25 towards his fare. "As I listened to them," Sam said, "I began to see the reality of Africa as the 'answer continent'."

At Oxford Sam also got to know trade unionists in the car factories who were aiming to cure class war. He travelled with them all over Britain. He was invited to other countries in Europe. He lived with miners' families, meeting communists, capitalists and even Prime Ministers. Sam used to ask himself, "How do I – Sam Pono from Queenstown – come to be sitting next to a Prime Minister who is interested to know what happened to me because he too has a family – as well as a Cabinet – with problems!"

Conrad Hunte, who had been Vice-Captain of the West Indies cricket team, invited him to go with him for some months to the West Indies. "I had always felt inferior to the West Indians", says Sam, "because I thought their control of the English language was better. When I told Conrad this we began to build trust together.

"He is a famous man, a real leader. I admired him and was tempted to copy him," Sam said. "He told me that it may take seven or ten years for a man to learn to be effective in the ideological battle for nations, that I can learn from anybody, but that, at the same time, I must stand on my own feet before God. I found that he, too, was ready to learn, even from me.

"This was a great lesson for me," Sam went on. "You can easily become a puppet, whether it's of another man, or of Marx, Mao or any leaders. We need the kind of independence in Africa where we are free not just of domination by whites but of dependence on other men. Then we will have people who can be trusted to do what is right."

Before he went to the West Indies Sam studied the history of the slave trade. "It was painful to learn that not only had the whites carried the slaves across the Atlantic, but that we Africans had sold our brothers to them. I had to accept the wrongs done by my own people, and not just blame others."

One incident in the West Indies sticks in Sam's mind. "We were in St. Vincent and a meeting was announced featuring Conrad. I thought we should have some music and I needed an African drum to accompany me. In my search for this I met a young man. He wanted to know all about the liberation struggle in Africa, and was also interested in my own story which had many similarities with his. I quickly realised he was one of the leaders of Black Power. The walls of his room were covered with pictures of revolutionaries. We talked a lot. He got the point that personal change was necessary if real political, social or economical change were to be achieved. He saw that the root struggle is not racial but runs through every man. He talked honestly of the West Indies where independence brought quarrelling for power and privilege while the masses were not cared for." Before Sam left, that man's whole thinking had expanded.

"I found that these militants were interested in three things," Sam said. "A vision for a world where no one is left out, and where Africa could be a model of how men live together; a discipline of absolute moral standards which could give us the needed leadership; an individual independence which does not rely on other men.

"Through all these experiences I have learnt that the most

130

ordinary man can be used by God in an extraordinary way," Sam said.

What if every South African who travelled abroad decided to be so used? Would this change the world's picture of South Africa?

16. CHOICE

Not long ago I was at a meeting in the Transvaal. There were a hundred people present, black and white, businessmen, headmasters, students. They were considering what God wanted them to do in Southern Africa.

A white engineer spoke. The previous day there had been a terrible tragedy when a schoolbus had gone off the road and thirty children had died. The engineer said, "As I was asking God for guidance this morning my thoughts turned to that accident. Suddenly I realised that the first question which had flashed through my mind when I heard of it was, 'Were they black or white'? My unspoken assumption was that, if they were black, it would not be quite so bad".

He was deeply shaken. "Do I actually think like that?" he thought. He asked God to forgive his callousness and he asked the same of the Africans in the hall.

His honesty was painful but fruitful. Painful because everyone listening identified himself with what he heard. Some of the blacks told the engineer afterwards that they had reacted in exactly the same way, only in reverse.

It was fruitful because it brought reality in a situation where black and white rarely expose to each other what they really feel. There is often superficial politeness, but each side knows this masks fears and feelings that are hidden. So there is no real basis for trust.

Ireland taught me similar lessons. In Belfast I was talking with a friend called Gerry. He was everything that I was not – a Catholic, a Labour Party official and a man who had suffered from discrimination. I was a Protestant of the conservative establishment. We had come to know each other over a couple of years. I felt we were friends. But, one day, he said to me, "Peter, I want to ask you one thing: if it comes to the crunch, will you do what is right or just go along with your own crowd?"

It was a good point. Unless I could honestly say "yes" to the first part of that question there was no hope for real trust between us.

I have had to accept that in a country like Ireland where, for centuries, we have had two distinct communities with opposing interests, our instinctive reactions are now often totally opposite.

Take, for instance, the question of loyalty. With my background, a mention of the Royal Family, Trafalgar, Waterloo or the British Navy touches a chord of pride. It has nothing to do with conscious calculation. It is the result of upbringing and a thousand and one things bred into my bones. I know, now, however, that those same things can produce a violently opposite reaction in others.

Just deciding that I want to work with men of the opposite background does not automatically alter those reactions. They remain. We will always be different. But, *fortunately, that is not the issue.*

The issue is whether we are prepared to be honest about what goes on inside us? Are we prepared to hand over control to a higher authority and let our wills be crossed?

It is asking a lot. It is, perhaps, asking for everything. It is what Christ tells us to do. St. Paul calls it "cutting the nerve of our instinctive reaction through obeying the Spirit".

What, for instance, goes through us each day when we read in the paper or hear on the radio of yet another awful thing that "they" have done? What do we do with the fear that, unasked, springs up inside us? Or the bitterness? God does not promise to stop these feelings. He does say we need no longer be controlled by them.

In Northern Ireland I once asked this same friend, "Gerry, we hear a great deal about discrimination in jobs, housing and so on. What are the facts?" He was silent for a moment. Then he said, "Facts only confuse the issue. It is feelings that count. They are the real facts".

At first I laughed. It sounded a very Irish remark. It is, however, a most profound and helpful comment. For in Ireland each side can produce its own set of facts. They are all accurate and prove its own case to its entire satisfaction. One side will say, "Look at all we do *for* them". The other will say, "Look at all they do *to* us". Each will be correct.

An old Scots friend, who lived through our Irish turmoil for several years, said to me, "Peter, if you want to do anything about Northern Ireland you must start from the point that everything each side feels about the other is absolutely true".

That, again, is more than a clever aphorism. It is truth which few of us are yet prepared to grasp. We still spend our time proving how right *we* are and how wrong *they* are, when what is needed is to learn to turn enemies into friends.

We are reluctant to face the reality of hate and fear. We find it hard to accept that there are seeds of hatred in each of us, or that others can actually hate us. We say, "Oh, you must not feel like that!" The reality is that others *do* feel like that.

I once visited one of our most senior churchmen in Ireland, a man I hold in high regard. I was with a number of visiting friends from India. One was a young man who had been involved in guerilla war on the North East border of his country.

Twenty of his relatives had been killed. He himself had received training from the Chinese. Later he re-found his Christian faith. He talked of his experiences and how he had hated. The churchman broke in, "I don't think there is hatred here in Ireland. Fear, yes. Prejudice, yes. But not hatred".

There was a stunned silence among our visitors. They had been several weeks in Northern Ireland and had talked to many. If what they had heard was not hatred, what was it? But we in Ireland call ourselves a Christian country. We know it is not Christian to hate, therefore we persuade ourselves we do not hate. This stops us reaching the depth of what divides us from other men. Honesty about ourselves and about our countries seems an essential precursor to healing. How can God – or men – forgive us for something we will not admit exists?

As I write this men, black and white, are dying on Northern borders. Only yesterday a white businessman talked with me of the possibility of a "Beirut" in South African cities within six months.

People who, from the safety of thousands of miles away, would welcome violence are either naive or vicious. They seem to think that another Frelimo-type campaign would swiftly topple South Africa. A radically-minded coloured leader, who is totally committed to changing the system, said to me that Russia and China, while they might encourage guerilla-type movements, would not risk direct military involvement at such a distance. "That apart, the South African Government has the power and the will to handle violence from anywhere south of Egypt for a long time to come and urban civil war, if it develops, will lead to slaughter of unimagineable proportions. So an alternative way of achieving change is not just a matter of morality for us. It is a stark necessity for anyone who will look facts in the face," he said.

Is it realistic to look for such a "change factor"? One might also ask, "What else is"? A wise man said, "To expect a change in human nature may be an act of faith; to expect a change in human society without it is an act of lunacy".

The supreme naivety is to believe that replacing one system with another is enough. Or that grudgingly-given concessions alone will suffice. They won't. That is a blunt statement. But Ireland and a dozen other situations prove its truth. It is no answer to tinker with trappings without touching the "why" – why people hit out, why they hate, hurt, fear, exploit.

In the final analysis only the man who has the courage to experiment with an answer in his own life will ever believe that it can work for his country.

The men and women in this book are some who show that it can be done. Will enough in Southern Africa take up this challenge? Will others in other lands?

It is a matter of choice.